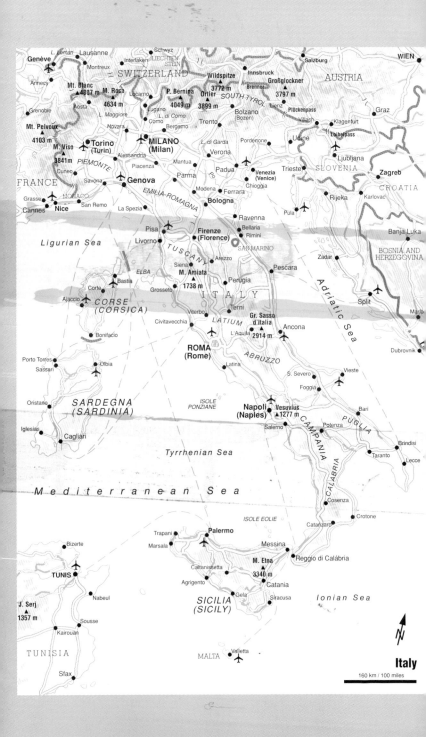

Italy

160 km / 100 miles

Welcome!

This guidebook combines the interests and enthusiasms of two of the world's best-known information providers: Insight Guides, who have set the standard for visual travel guides since 1970, and Discovery Channel, the world's premier source of non-fiction television programming.

 Insight Guides' correspondent, Joachim Chwaszca, has devised 16 itineraries to help you make the most of a short stay on the island. Included in the itineraries are tours of the islands of Sant'Antioco and San Pietro, a visit to Giuseppe Garibaldi's home on the Isla Caprera, and a special section on beaches. At the end of each tour is a selection of restaurants and places to stay. The itineraries section is complemented by the Practical Information section at the end of the book, which adds further restaurant recommendations as well as essential telephone numbers and useful tips.

Sardinia is the second-largest island in the Mediterranean. It is part of Italy, although some islanders wish it were not. Those familiar with mainland Italy will find many similarities, but they will also discover striking differences.

Over the past three decades, Sardinia has changed from a sleepy backwater dependent on sheep rearing and the production of pecorino cheese to a far more outward-looking region. There are disadvantages to this: the north coast has suffered as a result of mass tourism – without much of the revenue going into local pockets – and the Costa Smeralda has been taken over by an élite international jet set. Yet there are still many parts of this beautiful island which remain unspoiled, where travellers with a little initiative can make many discoveries of their own.

C O N T E N T S

Pages 8/9: enjoying Sardinia's strong winds

A History of Invasion

The bitter Sardinian maxim, *'Furat chi de su mare venit'* (Whoever comes by sea comes to rob us), more than adequately sums up the spirit of the island's history. With its prime location between Africa, Spain and Italy, Sardinia has suffered under many foreign invaders over the course of time. Caught up in violent conflicts between the great powers of the past, it has been overrun and conquered, exploited and plundered. In addition to its strategically significant position, rich ore deposits and fertile farmlands have made it even more attractive. Even today, those coming by sea have ulterior motives: as a NATO base and haven for international business concerns, Sardinia still finds itself used for military and industrial purposes. Tourists have come to plunder as well.

Since the Aga Khan 'discovered' the potential of the Costa Smeralda as a vacation paradise in the 1960s, each year larger numbers of tourists have arrived to occupy the beaches. But the

The columns of Tharros

Culture

Sardinians themselves have benefitted little. There is a still a stark contrast between the standard of living in the cities and the countryside and, as ever, the farmers are charged punishing rents for pasture lands.

History has not revealed the origins of the first people to settle Sardinia. However, on the basis of an abundance of archaeological finds, settlements dating back six millennia have been documented. Excavations support the claim that there existed a distinct Sardinian culture as

The ruins of Tharros

early as the fourth millennium BC. This was the Ozieri culture, named after the area in the north of the island which has yielded the most important finds. The Ozieri were an agricultural society whose most prominent feature was a death cult, striking evidence of which can still be seen today at numerous huge excavation sites on the island. A relatively high level of civilisation – though they apparently never developed the written word – was attained by another group known as the Nuragic, which flourished in the second millennium BC. Nuraghi is the name given to the barrel-shaped structures made of massive stone blocks which are still so well preserved on Sardinia today. Nobody knows exactly what their purpose was, but they were probably similar to medieval castles, serving as centres for communal activities in peacetime and as defences and refuges in times of war.

In the first millennium BC, a gradual, and at first quite peaceful, influx of Phoenician tradespeople began. Trading settlements, or colonies, were founded by this cultural group from the African coast, and were situated primarily in the southern part of Sardinia. For several centuries, the colonial rulers, whose main interest was the ore mines in the region of Iglesienti, remained on good terms

11

with the indigenous population. This situation prevailed until the 6th century BC, when newly founded Carthage, acting as the colonies' protector, took the island by force. This act of aggression ushered in 2,500 years of oppression for the Sardinian populace.

Bread Basket and Naval Base

The Carthaginian invaders used the island as both bread basket and base for their marine fleet. With the subjugation of the islanders, for the most part corralled in the economically depressed mountains while the invaders dominated the coastal regions and the south-west, the foundations were laid for a herding tradition which exists to this day. Remarkable remains from this period can be found at Tharros, on the Sinis peninsula, once a magnificent trading port. However, just 300 years later, the Carthaginians were ousted by the Romans who annexed Sardinia in 238 BC, and Sardinia changed masters. The Nuragic from the mountains allied themselves with their earlier enemies, the Carthaginians, and mounted a bitter resistance. In so doing, they developed specialised guerrilla tactics which they employed relentlessly, demonstrating to the Roman commanders the limitations of their own strategy, which was based on open warfare.

In general, the indigenous population remained recalcitrant throughout the entire period of Roman occupation, and proved a source of annoyance for the power-obsessed empire. Thus, Sardinia, whose people were railed against on the mainland as difficult and obstinate, became a place to exile Roman officers unwilling to toe the political line, or whose outlook was 'tarnished' by Christianity. As a result, the island was rapidly Christianized, a process accomplished elsewhere, albeit less speedily, with the gradual spread of the Latin language.

Despite the difficulties encountered by the foreign generals in subduing the population, the cities of the province were architecturally reshaped according to the requirements of the Romans. Numerous bridges, amphitheatres and private residences were erected. Street networks were extended and improved. In the year 27 BC, the first Roman city was founded at Turris Libisonis. At this time, Sardinians were first granted the civic rights of Roman citizens.

In the subsequent centuries, Sardinia's fortunes reflected the decay of the Roman Empire. The island was left to its own devices for the most part, but its infrastructure was seriously weakened by predatory attacks launched by invading Vandals, constantly recurring outbreaks of malaria, and uninterrupted incursions by seagoing pirates. With the Byzantine conquest, in the year 534, Sardinia fell victim to assaults from Islamic intruders. The total collapse of all central organisation, the decay of the irrigation system, and economic crisis was accompanied by a restructuring of the island's administration by Byzantium. Four *giudicati* were established in Cagliari, Torres, Arborea and Gallura, each under the political, administrative and judicial control of a *Giudice*. This was an hereditary office which, with the dissolution of the Byzantine

Empire, was assumed by the Sardinian aristocracy. A strictly hier-archical and feudalistic societal structure arose, in which only high ranking families with large land-holdings and significant numbers of livestock retained power. At the bottom of the pyramid were the farmers, without property or civil rights, but obliged to pay high tributes to their overlords. Their position was not exactly an enviable one, but it was better than it had been when the Romans were in control.

Fear of the Crescent

For many centuries, the danger of Muslim invasion was ever present, especially after the Moors conquered southern Spain in AD 711. But a Muslim Sardinia would have been accompanied by a re-structuring of the entire European balance of power. When Arab troops stormed the coastal areas around Cagliari in the year 1015, Pope Benedict VIII called upon the rising trading powers of Genoa and Pisa for help against the infidel. In 1016, the Islamic invaders were driven from the island. However, the assistance of the northern Italian sea republics was by no means disinterested. Soon after the Christian victory, the Sardinian aristocracy found itself sharing power and position with Pisans and Genoese.

But the rivalry between the two city states made the creation of a central, sovereign island government all the more difficult. The Genoese threw their weight behind the *giudicato* of Oristano whose leader, Barisone d'Arborea, was proclaimed king of Sardinia in 1164. But this was not the end of the matter: rioting and unrest, corruption and exhausting wars of attrition led to the intrusion of yet another foreign master at the close of the 13th century.

In 1297, Pope Boniface VIII turned Sardinia over to the kingdom of Aragon in northern Spain. At first, the climate of unrest continued unabated. The newly designated King of Sardinia, James II, did not much concern himself with his new colony. The rule of the Pisans and Genoans did not really end until the Aragonese Prince Alfonso defeated the Pisan forces and landed on Sardinia in 1323, supported by the *giudice* of Arborea, the last of the remaining judiciaries. Later, the Sardinians would seriously regret this alliance, as the Spanish outdid all previous foreign masters in terms of exploitation and tyranny. The Sardinians' battles of resis-tance filled the next 150 years, during which two folk heroes still

The Amphitheatre at Nora

honoured today made their mark on history, the Arborean *giudice* Mariano IV, and his daughter Eleonora. To the latter, the island owes the *Carta di Logu*, a book of criminal and civil law Eleonora published in 1392 and which was still in use in the 19th century.

Spanish rule and Unification

In 1478, the Spanish won a decisive victory over the indigenous rebels, and began resettling the island with their own people – particularly Catalan immigrants in the town of Alghero. With Spanish rule – under the combined houses of Aragon and Castile – came the long arm of the Inquisition. During the colonial period, which lasted almost 300 years, conditions on the island deteriorated. The contrast between city and countryside grew, the oppressive poverty experienced by the herdsmen and tenant farmers who had migrated to the mountains increased, and the function of the 'parliamentary assembly' degenerated to determining the amounts of tributes to be paid by Sardinians. Defiance and bitterness spread through the population. Those outside the pale created their own laws, and banditry became more endemic. As on Sicily, the Mafia came to the fore during the reign of Spanish oppression, developing

The Temple of the Sardus pater

a closed society with its own codex, the 'Laws of the Macchia'.

Foreign domination did not come to an end until the Spanish Wars of Succession, in which France, Austria and England were also embroiled. In 1708, the Spanish viceroy was driven out by the English and Austrians, and in 1713, the island was ceded to the House of Habsburg. Only seven years later this decision was revised, and Sardinia then came under the jurisdiction of the Northern Italian Dukes of Savoy-Piedmont.

But, with the removal of the Spanish, conditions did not improve. As reflected in a report from the first viceroy, the Baron of Saint-Remy, the 'criminal energy' seemed to pervade the air of Sardinia itself: 'The nobility is poor, the country miserable and depopulated, the inhabitants indolent and without any occupation, and the air is very unhealthy. The depravities to which these people mostly tend are thievery, murder, and fraud.' These prevailing conditions did not bode well for the island's new ruler

Mill stone at Su Nuraxi

nor for state unity. Not least among the problems he faced was language. The lower classes communicated in Sardinian, aristocrats spoke Castilian, but the new rulers used Italian. Efforts were made to confront the island's oppressive poverty by domesticating herds, settling Ligurian farmers in depopulated areas and restructuring the island's administration. But in the face of centuries-old abuse, these reforms could do very little.

All things considered, the island was ripe for a revolution. However, when French troops landed on Sardinia in 1793, they were routed and forced to flee by an ad hoc Sardinian force, who thus demonstrated their loyalty to the House of Piedmont. But this loyalty was not repaid: after their requests for direct involvement in government were denied, the disappointed Sardinians responded by expelling Piedmontese officials. Their rebellion was short-lived, but demands for self-government and the creation of a parliament were mounting. However, another 50 years passed before the abolition of feudalism.

In 1847 the unification of Sardinia and Piedmont was proclaimed and in 1861 the island became part of the newly unified Italian state, under Victor Emanuel II.

During World War I, thousands of Sardinians died for their country, and the *Brigata Sassari* became a symbol of courage. But the political demands formulated after the war by disillusioned soldiers who formed the Partito Sardo d'Azione – the Sardinian Action Party – in 1921 were to prove another kind of battlefield. Greater autonomy and equal rights were the issues, but Mussolini quashed all attempts to gain independence, although he made funds available for development projects. It was not until after World War II that Sardinia, for the first time since the age of the Ozieri, became an autonomous region guaranteed at least some measure of self-government, under the Sardinian Statute of 1948. More than half a century later, the Sardinian dream of total independence has still not been realised.

The water temple of Santa Christina

Historical Highlights

350,000BC First evidence of human settlements.

13,000BC Finds in Corbeddu Cave dating from this time are among the oldest human artefacts discovered on a Mediterranean island.

c 6000BC First cultures emerge.

6000–3000BC Sardinian obsidian tools, found in the Mediterranean area, are evidence of extensive trade contact.

c 1800BC The Nuragic build fortresses, water temples and graves.

c 1000BC The Phoenicians establish themselves on the coast.

540BC Phoenicians/Carthaginians solidify their positions and push the Nuragic population into the highlands. Cultivation of cereals and mining of ore.

238BC Sardinia becomes part of the Roman Empire, which founds cities and builds roads.

AD330 Coastal areas Christianised; first churches erected.

455 Sardinia is a Vandal province.

534 The Byzantine Empire conquers the island and Christianity makes further inroads.

c 704 Arab seafarers repeatedly plunder the coasts.

c 900 The four *giudicati* of Torres, Gallura, Cagliari and Arborea are formed for protection and centralised administration. Byzantine generals relieved of power.

1015 Allied with Genoa and Pisa, Sardinia repels the Arabs.

11th c Genoa strengthens its influence in the north, Pisa in the south. By 1298, three of the *giudicati* have been dissolved.

1284 Pisa is defeated and loses its influence.

1297 Sardinia granted to House of Aragon.

1324 Spanish rule begins.

1325 Ruling families from Italian mainland lose influence.

1388 A Spanish viceroy rules. The last *giudicato,* Arborea, holds out until 1478.

1392 Eleonora d'Arborea decrees the renowned *Carta di Logu*. Mountain herdsmen and farmers live by their own code.

1708 The Spanish Wars of Succession bring Austrian rule.

1720 The dukes of Piedmont-Savoy become kings of Sardinia. Italian becomes the *lingua franca*. The French Revolution sparks rebellions which are put down.

1798–1814 The Savoyans are driven out of Turin by Napoleon, and retreat into exile in Sardinia.

1839 Feudal system abolished.

1847 Sardinia and Piedmont form an alliance. Sardinia pays a heavy price for the unification of Italy. The independence campaign consumes the country; many Sardinians die in the fight for liberation.

1918 The bravery of the *Brigata Sassari* changes the way the mainland Italians view Sardinia, and becomes the core of a post-war movement for autonomy. Emilio Lussu and Antonio Gramsci are the main protagonists.

1930 Fascism wins followers on Sardinia. Coal mining in Sulcis is developed to help the economy.

1948 Sardinia made an autonomous region of the republic.

1960s Petrochemical development and the opening up of the island to tourism.

1970s–1980s Spectacular kidnappings and the Costa Smeralda jet set make the tabloid headlines.

1985 Francesco Cossiga from Sassari is elected President of the Italian Republic.

1990 Cagliari is one of the venues in the soccer World Cup.

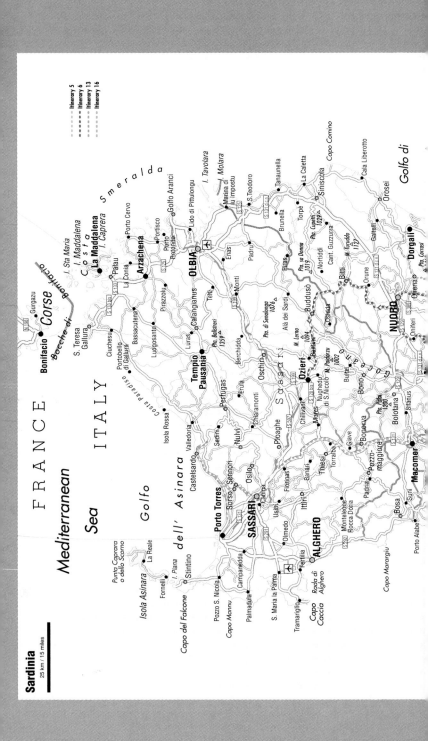

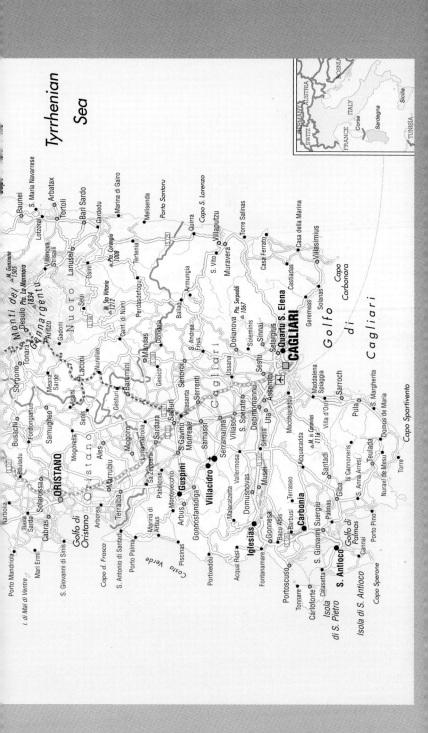

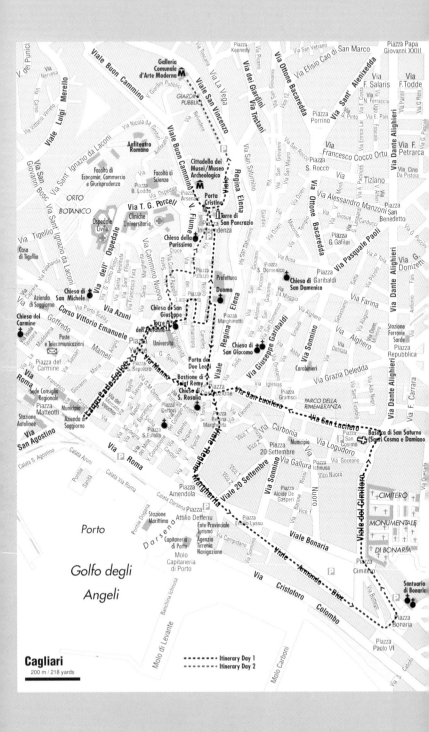

Cagliari

200 m / 218 yards

- - - - - Itinerary Day 1
.... Itinerary Day 2

CAGLIARI

Cagliari (pronounced Calyar-ee) has a little bit of everything: the cosmopolitan character of a port city, the luxuries of an Italian shopping mecca, Spanish ambience in the old quarter and the villagey character of a small Sardinian town. It is a pleasant place with a warm atmosphere, open and accessible, backlit by the wonderful Mediterranean sun. 'Strange and rather wonderful, not a bit like Italy' is how D.H. Lawrence described the capital of the island, set atop its 10 hills.

Cagliari is one of the oldest cities in Europe, a statistic of which its inhabitants are justly proud. And though for centuries it was subject to a parade of foreign powers, it has never lost its prized significance as a trading port. Founded by the Phoenicians, the name of the city stems from the Spanish *kalaris* or *karali*, which goes back to a still older root word, meaning 'rocky place', quite a suitable epithet considering the limestone hills of Castello and Capo Sant' Elia.

Today, almost one Sardinian in six lives in or around Cagliari and the city's population tops 212,000. Pressing economic problems stemming from the decline of agriculture and animal husbandry are behind the islanders' flight to the city. Roughly one third of the population is unemployed. But despite the prevailing situation on the island, Cagliari has an air of dignity, giving the lie to the Italians' contemptuous tag: 'hide-clothed Sardinians'. When Rome was still a sleepy provincial town, Cagliari was already a flourishing trade centre and it is still the place where most new industries on the island choose to locate. Driving around the city is best left to the locals who can make sense of the one-way system, poor signage and austere parking regualations. Wherever possible see the town on foot and use the public transport system. Cagliari has some of the best restaurants on the island and a small selection of hotels, but make sure you book ahead to make reservations in the summer season.

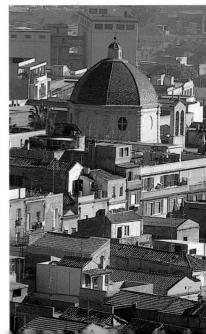

View of Cagliari

Old Quarter Walking Tour and dinner at the Marina

A day in Cagliari: a walking tour of the historic quarter, Castello, and dinner in a small fish restaurant near the port.

We begin our stroll along the lower segment of the **Boulevard Largo Carlo Felice**, in the area of the harbour and the shady, heavily trafficked **Piazza Matteotti**. The plaza is named after the socialist politician, Giacomo Matteotti, who was murdered in 1924 as a result of his speech, 'The Rule of Force', following the

The curving staircase to the Bastion di Saint-Remy

election victory of the fascists. Behind us lies the harbour of Cagliari, enlarged in the 19th century, with the **Molo di Sanità** and the **Stazione Marittima**, which primarily serve ferries arriving from Civitavecchia, Naples, Palermo and Tunis. Located before us on the left is the **Stazione Ferrovie dello Stato**, and directly on the corner of the Largo is the 19th-century neo-Gothic **Municipio** (City Hall). On the other corner, the **Via Roma** begins, with the luxury department store **La Rinascente**.

We begin our tour the Italian way with an *espresso* or a *cappuccino*. Behind city hall on the corner of Largo you will find a bar where you can fortify yourself with a *brioche*. Then we will

22

Boulevard Largo Carlo Felice and the harbour

head slowly up the Largo, a street where many of the shopkeepers and residents are Africans. Here, you will find copies of designer goods, from Vuitton bags and Ray-Ban sunglasses to scarves from Ferre or Versace. At the end of this lively boulevard is the **Piazza Yenne** with its Roman column. This marks the beginning of the Roman road from Cagliari to Porto Torres, the present-day super-highway Carlo Felice (SS131). In front of it is the statue of the Viceroy Carlo Felice, who commissioned the road which bears his name, gesturing in the opposite direction to his highway.

We saunter along between itinerant street sellers and various banking establishments guarded by scowling, heavily armed security guards. Halfway up the street, and hidden on the right side, is the Chiesa Sant'Agostino, a Renaissance church erected in 1580, which you enter from the Largo through a garden ornamented with sculptures. Once out on the Largo again, you will come across Via Manno. Resist for now the attractions of this street, which you would be better off saving for the late afternoon when it becomes a stage on which the inhabitants of Cagliari parade, decked out in the latest fashions. Instead, now we follow the steps straight ahead which lead us past the small **Market Hall** and directly into **Castello**, the old quarter.

At the top of the stairs, the view extends over the Largo Carlo Felice, down to the harbour and on out over the sea. The heart of old Cagliari still beats behind the **Torre dell'Elefante**, the former rulers' quarter of Castello. The Torre dell'Elefante, a masterpiece of mediaeval fortification, its stones fitted together without mortar, dates from 1307 and was erected by a Pisan master-builder. Over the long course of the centuries it has stood as the emblem of this ancient city. To the left,

In the Castello quarter

next to the portcullis, the origin of the tower's name becomes clear. A small stone elephant on a plinth looks calmly out over the bustling modern city. Several of the old craftsmen in this area still maintain little shops while cabinetmakers and cobblers ply their trades under naked lightbulbs. Emblematic of the area is the laundry of the Cagliarians, hung out to dry above the streets of the old quarter, a section of the city, part of which is, unfortunately, becoming rather dilapidated. Some of the façades of its history-rich palaces are decaying, but there are numerous efforts at preserving or renovating the old buildings.

Turn right, after the tower, then left into the Via Duomo. On our right lies the **Duomo**, the **Cattedrale Santa Maria del Castello** (Cathedral of St Maria), originally built in Pisan-Romanesque style. Don't be misled by the façade – it was actually erected in 1933. The church itself was built in the 13th century – only the belfry and the beams supporting the main doorway still remain – and remodelled for the first time in the 14th century. Inside is a splendid pulpit from the cathedral in Pisa, which was presented as a gift to the city of Cagliari in 1312. Additions to the façade, based on the old Pisan-Romanesque plans, have not incorporated any elements of the excessively ornamental baroque style which prevails in the interior.

Outside the cathedral on the **Piazza Palazzo** cars are wedged into the parking lot in front of the **Prefettura**, housed in a splendid 18th-century building which was once the Royal Palace. If we go past the Prefettura, towards the Piazza Indipendenza, we will come to the **Torre di San Pancrazio**, the Elephant Tower's twin, which is open to the public during the day. It offers the best view over the Poetto beach, the eastern section of the city, and the Golfo degli Angeli. Near the tower lies the palm-festooned Terrazza Umberto I. With its expanse of open ground, at the edge of the crowded old quarter, this plaza is without doubt one of the most beautiful in Italy. From its balustrades, you have a fantastic view over almost the entire city as well as of the mountainous interior. From the plaza we retrace our steps past the Duomo to the **Bastion di Saint-Remy**. In the early 18th century, after 400 years of Spanish rule, the Baron de Saint-Remy became the first Piedmontese viceroy of Sardinia, and made his name by enlarging the island's fortifications. The former 'reception room' of the *Casteddus*, as it is called by native Cagliarians, today serves as an ideal course for young skateboarders.

Descending by way of a curving staircase, we now continue directly on to the **Piazza Constituzione**, from where we turn right into the **Via Manno** in order to participate in the late-afternoon promenade-cum-fashion show of the Cagliarians. For the Italians, this *passagiata* consists principally of 'seeing and being seen'. In the Via Manno, you can find everything required for good Italian-style *gioia di vivere*. Above all, this is a place to do your shopping. It is here you will find bags, clothing and shoes, all of good quality. Carry on along the Via Manno until you reach the familiar broad Largo Carlo Felice, where we come to the end of our tour.

Where to go for dinner? A good suggestion is to continue down Largo Carlo Felice then take a left-hand turn into the historic harbour quarter known as **Marina**. Here, at Via Sardegna 78, you will find the fish restaurant **Da Lillicu** (tel: 070 652 970) where you can dine on indigenous fish specialities served atop bare marble tables at reasonable prices. Pasta dishes are to be had here only upon protracted demand, and even then only *spaghetti al burro* (with butter) or *spaghetti al pomodoro* (with tomato sauce). If you have a good appetite and want a hearty appetiser, try the *frutti di mare* (seafood platter). An outstanding dish is *cozze* (mussels) cooked in the restaurant's own style. When it comes to choosing the main dish, you will see the day's catch. It is a matter of personal taste whether you drink the *bianco* house wine, the *vermentino* (Aragosto, for example) or perhaps an Ichnusa beer.

If so much fish does not appeal, you could try the **Italia** at Via Sardegna 30 (tel: 070 657 987). This restaurant offers as an alternative a rich selection of Sardinian and Italian dishes, as well as a wine cellar famous throughout the city. A final *caffé* under the arcades of the Via Roma (which runs parallel to Sardegna), surrounded by the sounds of Cagliari after dark, will round off your day in fitting style.

Along the waterfront on the Via Roma

Cagliari Cultural and Gourmet Tour

Full day in Cagliari: in the morning, the Museo Archeologico and the Galleria Communale d'Arte Moderna, plus a visit to the Basilica di San Saturno; shopping in the Via Manno; an array of authentic restaurants to choose from in the evening.

In the tried and tested Italian manner, begin your day with a double breakfast. Soon after getting up drink your first *cappuccino* of the day just as an eye opener. Your second breakfast is consumed once you are out and about standing up in a street-corner bar: *spremuta* from fresh-squeezed oranges, *caffé* or *cappucino* and, of course, along with this, a *pasta con crema*.

Entrance to the Castello in the Old Quarter

The old quarter of Cagliari is not really penetrable by car. From the hotels Italia or the Quattro Mori, you can go by foot to the Cittadella dei Musei. Walk up the Largo Carlo Felice and then via the stairway to the little Market Hall. A quick peep inside can't hurt before taking in the archaeological and artistic treasures in the museum. One look at the fresh catch of the day, and you will be looking forward with anticipation to your evening meal. Enter the old quarter, called **Castello**, through the Torre dell'Elefante, then keep to the left since the way leads along the fortification walls from the Bastione Santa Croce to the Chiesa Santa Maria del Monte. By way of the Via dei Genovesi, you reach the Via Lamarmora, the **Piazza Indipendenza** and the **Torre di San Pancrazio**.

The **Piazza Arsenale**, located in the fortified circle behind the Torre di San Pancrazio, shelters the **Cittadella dei Musei**, the former castle fortress housing the city's museum complex. The

The graceful descent to the Bastion di Saint-Remy

various museums in the Cittadella spans all eras of Sardinian history, managing to represent both the old and the new in equal proportions, but the major event is the **Museo Archeologico Nazionale** (open Tues–Sun 9am–8pm; admission charge) which presents a great opportunity to prepare yourself for all the sites of historical interest on the island. Portrayals of the human figure from the period of the **Nuraghi** (from around the 3rd millennium BC) demonstrate the powerful expressive urge of a civilisation seemingly so far removed from our own. Here you can admire gods, warriors, votive lamps in the form of boats, as well as ceramics and weapons from the golden age of Nuragic culture. The high points in this section are the Bronzetti Nuragici. The Phoenician epoch is also well covered. The museum houses finds from Nora, Sulcis, Tharros and Monte Sirai. The Carthaginian and Roman periods are also explored, from the oldest inscriptions in Sardinian to ancient vases and kitchen utensils. Medieval and Early Christian artefacts are also on display.

The Cittadella dei Musei also houses the **Pinacoteca Nazionale** (National Art Gallery; open Tues–Sun 9am–8pm; admission charge) which is well worth seeing if you haven't exhausted yourself with archaeology. Also contained in the complex is the **Museo d'Arte Orientale Stefano Cardu** (open Tues–Sun summer 9am–1pm, 4–8pm; winter 9am–1pm, 3.30–7.30pm; admission charge), which contains Chinese and Siamese objets d'art, and the **Mostra di Cere anatomiche** (open Tues–Sun 9am–1pm, 4–7pm; admission charge) which displays 23 realistic anatomical wax models based on originals made by Clemente Susini in 1803.

But there is more art awaiting you: at the foot of the Piazza Arsenale, walking downhill into Viale Regina Elena, you will come to the pleasant **Giardini Pubblici** (Public Gardens), in the middle of which lies the **Galleria Communale d'Arte Moderna** (Gallery of

From sole to octopus—the selection seems endless

Modern Art; open summer 9am–1pm; 5–9pm; winter Wed–Mon 9am–1pm, 3.30–7.30pm; admission charge; www.collzioneingrao.it). This is an essential visit, if only to see Francisco Ciusa's sculptural masterpiece *La Madre dell'Ucciso*. A leading turn-of-the-century Sardinian sculptor, Ciusa gained international recognition and was honoured at the 1907 Venice Biennale.

After this, you will need a little time to catch your breath, something best accomplished in a little 'vertical' bar beneath the plane trees. Here in the south, midday is siesta time, and everything gravitates into the *ristorantes* or home to *mamma*, so you will probably have the bar to yourself. If you would prefer a *ristorante*, for a good but expensive midday meal, try **Flora**. Located at Via Sassari 45 (tel: 070 664 735), it offers typical Sardinian cuisine – try the pasta alla bottarga. To take the shortest route, turn into the Via Mammeli from the Piazza Yenne (near the Torre dell'Elefante), then branch off to the left into the Via Sassari. An alternative plan is to go into an *alimentari* and order a *panino* and perhaps read D.H. Lawrence's *Sea and Sardinia*, while relaxing in the shade.

To round off the siesta hour have a *caffé* along with a refreshing *acqua minerale* under the arches of the Via Roma with their splendid façades, shaded by red awnings. Here you could laze away the time or if you have any energy left you are then going in the right direction to take a pleasant walk along the seafront, on Viale Armando Diaz or Viale Bonaria, where you will find Piazza Paolo VI and the famous white staircase leading to **Basilica di Nostra Signora di Bonaria** (open summer 6.30am–noon, 4.30–7.30pm, winter 6.30am–noon, 4–6.30pm; www.nsdibonaria.it), the largest church in Sardinia, erected in 1704 to watch over sailors at sea. Keep walking into Viale Cimitero and you will come to the beautiful Piazza San Cosimo and the **Basilica di San**

Saturno (open Mon–Sat 9am–1pm). Built over a Roman necropolis, this was the first Christian church in Sardinia, and was reopened after 20 years of restoration work.

When the shops reopen at 4pm, you might like to browse. Walk along Via San Lucifero towards the Piazza Constituzione, and start with the less-expensive end of the market. On your right just before you reach the piazza are the shops of **Via Garibaldi** but the main shopping street is the **Via Manno** *(see Tour 1)*, on the other side of the piazza, which has designer and upmarket chain stores in which to browse. Along the way, you will notice the artful marriage of modern design and traditional architecture in the interiors of these shops. Appropriate headgear for men is part of the summer ambience of Italy. The Martello family's concern, *Cappelli e Berretti,* is a haberdashery with an original interior dating from the turn of the 20th century, located on the Via Sassari. This is, quite simply, the *Borsalino* shop!

For a more vibrant shopping experince head for the great market hall in **Mercato San Benedetto** (open Mon–Fri morning), Via Cocco Ortu, which is best reached by taxi. The market sells household goods and food. If it's a snack you're after, you can obtain everything your heart desires in the shops between the **Mercato Vecchio**, the **Via Baylle** and the **Via Sardegna** in the **Marina Quarter**. Here, old men will offer you little bags of mussels, and farmers from the environs of Cagliari sell their *spinnosi* – small spiny artichokes. The cheese shops in the Via Sardegna are beyond compare with countless variations of *pecorino, dolce sardo* and other delicacies.

The amazing variety of gourmet foods will draw you into delicatessen shops such as the **Salumeria Vaghi** (Via Baylle). Here you will find wild boar ham and smoked venison, first-class wine, *mirto* spirits and *pasta fresca*. Naturally, there's also dried fish, the *baccallà* or *bottariga di cefalo* (caviar). For a Sardinian **wine-tasting** session, the selection of the *Enoteca Cagliaritana* is recommended. It is located across from the small market hall on the Piazza Yenne.

After all these culinary pleasures, it may be difficult to even think about your evening meal, but perhaps, after all your walking and sightseeing, you will have built up an appetite. This time your meal will not be cheap, but it is almost certain to be enjoyable. Try any of the places recommended on page 31, and you will have a meal to remember. Some, like Lo Scoglio and Sa Cardiga e su Schironi are a little out of town, but well worth the trip.

Devotional figurines in the Via Manno

Accommodation

Even though Cagliari is by far the largest and most significant city on Sardinia, it does not have much in the way of accommodation. If you only want to spend only a few days here book rooms at a hotel near the centre of town. There are few enough even of these centrally located hotels. Instead of the state-regulated prices, which in Italy are posted on every hotel door, price *categories* are offered here as an aid to orientation. Throughout Sardinia, you are best off making reservations in advance by telephone, since many hotels are booked up (or closed in winter) and a call can save you time and frustration. The Cagliari code prefix is 070.

REGINA MARGHERITA ☆☆☆☆☆
Viale Regina Margherita 44
Tel: 670342; fax: 668325
www.hotelreginamargherita.com

MEDITERRANEO ☆☆☆☆
Lungomare Colombo 46
Tel: 301271; fax: 301274
www.hotelmediterraneo.net

CAESAR'S HOTEL ☆☆☆
Via Darwin 2
Tel: 340750; fax: 340755
www.caesarshotel.it

CALAMOSCA SUL MARE ☆☆☆
Viale Calamosca 50
Tel: 371628; fax: 370346
www.hotelcalamosca.it

ITALIA ☆☆☆
Via Sardegna 31
Tel: 660410; fax: 650240
email: hotelitalia@tiscali.it

PANORAMA ☆☆☆
Viale Diaz 231
Tel: 307691; fax: 305413
www.hotelpanorama.it

QUATTRO MORI ☆☆
Via G M Angioy 27
Tel: 668535; fax: 666087
www.hotel4mori.it

Sardinian Easter pastries

Restaurants

Among the resident gourmets of Sardinia, Cagliari is considered a paradise. In and around the city there are a great many very good places to eat, listed below is just a selection of the very best. It is impossible in such an area to list every single establishment worthy of a visit and you should try some of the numerous small restaurants where the locals go for lunch. Around the Via Baylle at the Mercato Vecchio you will also find excellent delicatessens for snacks or gifts.

DEL CORSARO✭✭✭✭
Viale Regina Margherita 28
Tel: 370295

FLORA✭✭✭✭
Via Sassari 45
Tel: 664735

LO SCOGLO✭✭✭✭
Capo S. Elia, Loc.
Calamosca
Tel: 371927

OTTAGONO✭✭✭✭
Lungomare Poetto
Tel: 541719

SA CARDIGA E SU SCHIRONI✭✭✭✭
Capoterra, SS195
10km (6 miles) from Cagliari
Tel: 71652/71613

ANTICA HOSTARIA✭✭✭
Via Cavour 60
Tel: 665870

ITALIA✭✭✭
Via Sardegna 30
Tel: 657987

PAPPA E CITTI✭✭✭
Viale Trieste 66
Tel: 665770

ST REMY✭✭✭
Via Torino 16
Tel: 657377

AL PORTO✭✭
Via Sardegna 44
Tel: 663141

CRACKERS✭✭
Corso V. Emanuele II 195
Tel: 653912

DA LILLICU✭✭
Via Sardegna 78
Tel: 652970

SERAFINO✭
Via Lepanto 6
Tel: 651795

Vehicle Rental

You will find that almost all of the car rental firms are represented at the Elmas Airport. To have a car waiting for you at the airport simply reserve in advance from your airport of departure or over the Internet. The rates vary, with and without kilometre restrictions, and there are also weekend package rates.

Most rental firms maintain additional offices in other Sardinian cities, where you are usually able to drop off cars. You will find the addresses you need at the back of this book *(see page 104)* and additional vehicle rental information is available from most hotel reception desks or from the Internet.

Tour **3**

Phoenician Nora to Villaperuccio

From Cagliari, to the Phoenician city of Nora; hike through the dunes on Capo Spartivento; return via Teulada and the fairies' houses at Villaperuccio, or continue on to Sant'Antioco.

Leave the motorised chaos of Cagliari, centred upon **Piazza Matteotti** and the **Via Roma**, as quickly as possible, following the signs at the train station to the left towards **Pula** and SS195. The large bridge at the mouth of the **S. Gilla lagoon** is a popular fishing spot. The Sardinians pursue their favourite sport here, using permanently installed rods and large rectangular nets. This stretch of Sardinian coast is called the **Golfo degli Angeli**. With its landscape punctuated by refineries and tanker moorings surrounded by salt-encrusted flood plains, it is quite an unusual scene. However, the silhouette of the city – from Capo Sant' Elia to Castello, and on to the cupola of the Cathedral – is worth a backward look.

Drive on to **Sarróch**, rapidly leaving behind the gigantic petrochemical complex. Not far beyond the refineries, a little road branches off into a village which offers a welcome alternative to the SS195. At **Villa San Pietro** you will again enter the main road, and see **Pula** in the distance. **Villa Santa Maria** in Pula is a splendid neoclassical building, built in 1838, which is close to the

Nora, Chia and Teulada

10 km / 6 miles

Museo Archeologico (open summer 9am–8pm; admission charge) where all the Punic and Roman findings from Nora are kept – a good preparation for a visit to the nearby necropolis.

The ancient Phoenician/Carthaginian/Roman city of **Nora** now lies before you on a spit of land surrounded by sea. The archaeological site (open 9am–sunset) thought to comprise the oldest urban settlement on the island, was discovered in the 1950s.

You can still get a good feel for the ancient city from viewing the ruined temples, mosaics and amphitheatre. The little pilgrimage church of **Sant'Efisio** outside the city is the goal of the great *Sagra Sant'Efisio* held in Cagliari on 1 and 2 May.

Beaches are the reason for being on the **Pineta**, the strip of coastline between Pula and Chia. Here you will find the **Grand Hotel Chia Laguna**, which is famous throughout Italy. There is also a stylish pool at the Is Molas Golf, and an 18-hole golf course open to non-residents, but for a high daily fee. If lying on the beach for hours does not appeal to you, you may decide to drive on further, to **Chia**, and admire its Saracen tower. Archaeologists and experienced antiquarians among you will note the remains of another old Phoenician city.

Others will detect little more than a couple of rocky fragments, and waste no time getting back to the coast for a cooling swim and a hike through the towering white sand dunes of **Capo**

In ancient Phoenician Nora

Spartivento. The bays here are not readily accessible, and you must often walk for a while to reach your destination. But this part of the gulf is popular among professional surfers, who lend the bay local colour. Swimmers take note: the bay is lashed by strong winds in spring.

The coastal road to **Porto di Teulada** is the western stretch of the *Strada Panoramica*. Here the island presents a visual feast: sheer, craggy coastline glowing in rich earth tones, watchtowers, turquoise water, white beaches and blooming *màcchia*. And if you are enjoying the coast and not ready to go inland, you might take a little excursion to the **Isola di Sant'Antioco**, which is connected to the mainland by a broad causeway.

Teulada, the next town inland, is internationally known for sculpture, and especially renowned for its Holy Friday celebrations known locally as Su Iscravamentu (the Un-nailing). Some 30km (18 miles) on is **Santadi**, famous for its *pecorino* cheese. Nearby at Villaperuccio is the **Necropli del Monte Essu**, with *domus de janas* (fairies' houses) set in a natural amphitheatre. In the nearby cave, the **Grotta Is Zuddas**, splendid nativity celebrations are staged.

Half Day Trip to Villasimius

From Cagliari, this tour takes you to the wonderful beaches of the east coast, includes a meal with a literary ambience and an area of local craftwork; choice of overnight stay or return trip.

No matter how tight your schedule is, a drive out from Cagliari can't be missed. The beaches of the south-east coast are, quite simply, the stuff of dreams. The waters along the headland are among the cleanest in the Mediterranean and their rich vegetation and marine life makes them popular with scuba divers.

This excursion begins on the SS125 in **Poetto** at the **Spiagga di Quartu**, only a few kilometres from the city centre. For some time Poetto has been *the* swimming beach of Cagliari. At the turn of the century there were great wooden bathing establishments, and orchestras played at summer festivals; today you will find snack bars and lidos where you can use shower and toilet facilities. Volleyball and windsurfing have as firm a foothold here as the countless street hawkers, without whom Poetto would not be a real Italian beach. Visitors with children will not want to miss Poetto, if only because of the *lunaparks* (funfairs).

At **Margine Rosso** – after the junction with the bypass road which leads directly to Elmas Airport – the landscape is transformed.

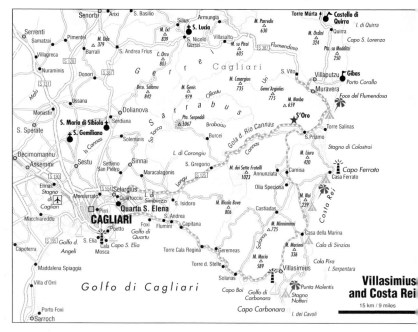

Villasimius and Costa Rei

15 km / 9 miles

Although in recent years the construction of holiday homes and hotels has escalated, it still has not tarnished the beauty of the area. In fact, several of the small villages seem to be withstanding all attempts to modernise them.

The road, which leads us past the coastal watchtowers of the Spanish and blooming *màcchia*, provides breathtaking views. Dusty little tracks twist down here and there in hairpin curves to small bays. Going uphill a few kilometres past **Solanas**, a fascinating view of the **Golfo di Carbonara** opens up ahead.

From here it is just a few kilometres to **Villasimius**. Only at Pentecost and in August should this town be avoided because of overcrowding. Otherwise, the village, with its dream-like beaches, is pleasant and quiet. Although there are a series of restaurants and hotels worth recommending in Villasimius, a favourite is the **Stella d'Oro**, located only a few metres from the main plaza. Since Ernst Jünger wrote his book on Sardinia, *By the Saracens' Tower*

The picturesque coast near Villasimius

in the 1950s, the Stella d'Oro has been a goal for literary pilgrims. Apart from its literary connotations, the food is highly recommended. Try the *malfatti*, ricotta with spinach dumplings, along with white wine and olives as an antipasto.

You could return to Cagliari via a circular route on the SS125, but an overnight stay in Villasimius is worthwhile; and if you have a bit more time you might also like to continue your drive via the **Costa Rei**, which is an ideal place for a stop-over to explore the Flumendosa estuary. **Muravera** is the biggest village in the area, renowned for the quality of its oranges. From here you can visit San Vito and Villaputzu, the nearby Pisan-Romanesque church of **San Nicola di Quirra** (dating from 1300), and the Castello di Quirra, with its breathtaking views. You may want to continue to **Torre Murta** where there are the reamains of a 3rd-millennium BC settlement, including a *domus de janas*. To return to Cagliari take the SS125, from where you will get some of the best views in southern Sardinia of the **Gola di Rio Cannas** gorge and **Monte dei Sette Fratelli** (Seven Brothers), a small range of mountains with peaks up to 1,000 metres (3,280 ft) high.

From Cagliari to Sassari

This excursion goes north from Cagliari via the Superstrada Carlo Felice, through the Marmilla Plain, and includes trips to the Nuraghi settlement of Su Nuraxi at Barumini, the water temple of Santa Cristina, and the Santa Trinità di Saccargia church.

This tour begins in southern Cagliari. It takes a while to fight your way through the city traffic and the continuous traffic jam of the Via Roma. Here **Cagliari** shows its less attractive side, and dire industrial buildings dominate the scene. Follow the signs for **Sassari** on the SS131 (Superstrada Carlo Felice). This road was built in the 1970s to link the two main cities, replacing the

Inside a Nuraghi fortress

ancient road which increased traffic had made inadequate. You will see the remains of this road as you approach Sassari on the highway, avoiding more than 40 sharp bends that used to be part of the journey. The drive takes you through the fertile lowlands of **Campidano**, especially beautiful in spring, but lovely at any time of the year. Exit the Carlo Felice at the turn-off for **Villamar**. There are signs now for Barumini as well as Su Nuraxi, and the road leads straight as an arrow to the mountains and the **Giara di**

Su Nuraxi at Barumini

Gesturi, where the wild giara horses are a protected breed. In order to get to Barumini you must take the SS197 road at Villasanta, passing the village of Villamar. Driving across the **Marmilla Plain** you head directly towards a large hill, known as *La Marmella* – the bosom – because of its symmetrical curves. Atop this hill, you can make out the ruins of fortifications marking a boundary between the old Sardinian judiciaries of Cagliari and Arborea – the 12th-century **Castello Las Plassas**. This beautiful region, with fields covered in wild flowers in spring, is home to a wide variety of birds, including the Sardinian partridge and the bee eater.

Before entering the village of **Barumini**, you will see the **Su Nuraxi** complex (open daily 9am–dusk; guided tours; entrance fee) about 1km (½ mile) to the west. This Nuraghi village, recently listed as a World Heritage Monument, is the most imposing ancient site on Sardinia. The oldest part of the fortress dates from 1500BC. An impressive central tower, framed by four still-intact corner towers, rises over a battlement itself some 5m (16ft) higher than the surrounding grounds. Around the fortified complex are residential quarters, erected in various phases and now excavated. The buildings have been partially reconstructed by archaeologists, who have been able to determine that the people here had ovens in which they baked the equivalent of today's *pane carasau*, or pitta bread. Round stone plates with an approximate diameter of 2m (7ft) served as a mill. The house of a stonecutter has also been identified, as well as a specially decorated structure, possibly the seat of a leader, and an assembly hall outfitted with seats. From the main tower you can make out over 60 round huts. Small streets and alleys, some equipped with steps, pass between these dwellings and interconnect the village. Nowhere else on Sardinia do you get a more immediate impression of the Nuragic culture. Retrace your steps to the Villasanta exit. You must cover a good 70km (43 miles) on the Carlo Felice before reaching your next des-

Santa Trinità di Saccargia

tination. On the way, you will pass **Sardara**, the best known thermal baths on Sardinia, which have also lent their name to a popular mineral water. A sign reading *Zona Arceologica,* posted just outside **Paulilatino**, on the stretch of the Carlo Felice between Oristano and Abbasanta, points the way to a site which you really must not omit from your itinerary. This is the **Il Pozzo di Santa Cristina** (open 8.30am–sunset; entrance fee), a water temple which dates from 1000BC. A triangular staircase – remarkable for the unbelievable precision of its construction – leads through the earth to a fountain situated several metres underground. The fountain is by far the most harmonious and perfect work of construction attempted during this period, and conveys, perhaps even more than the fortress towers or the *tombe dei giganti*, the high level of sophistication attained by the Nuragic. The **Museo Archeologico-Etnográfico** (open Tues–Sun daily) in the centre of town has a collection of finds from Santa Cristina. A short distance from the fountain stands the pilgrimage church of **Santa Cristina**, with the pilgrims' lodgings next to it. This has been a holy site for some 3,000 years, revered first by the Nuraghi, then by the Phoenicians and finally by the Christians.

Only 6km (4 miles) further north on the right-hand side of the SS131, stands the great tower of **Nuraghe Losa** (open daily 9am–sunset; entrance fee), which dates from an even earlier epoch. This is also an impressive construction, 13m (43ft) tall and well preserved, with ivy climbing up its ponderous walls. Stretching out before it, as in Barumini, are the living and assembly areas, although not quite as extensive here as in Su Nuraxi. The Nuraghe Losa is also accessible by foot, and offers a beautiful view over the surrounding landscape. The next Nuraghe is easy to find as it is well within view from the highway. Cut across the landscape of gently rolling hills around **Macomer**, the heart of the domestic cheese industry. Numerous archaeological finds here indicate that this region was settled particularly early on. Eleven kilometres (7 miles) past the small city of Bonorva, east of the Carlo Felice, is the **Nuraghe S. Antine** (open daily 9am–sunset; admission charge includes entrance to the museum), which appears so striking due to its black walls. The name itself means Saint Constantine, and the reference is to the Roman Caesar Constantine, who is especially revered on Sardinia. The central tower of the complex, 18m (59ft) tall and 15m (48ft) wide, is even more impressive than the tower at Nuraghe Losa. Locally, the gigantic fortress building is known as the 'house of the king', a fitting title. The large interior courtyard, its entrance guarded by watch niches, used to serve as an area for storing weapons. The defenders here were able to detect approaching forces by sound carried through acoustic canals.

Due to the perfect execution of such sophisticated structures it was assumed until quite recently that Nuragic culture dated from a period after the turn of the first millennium. However, the latest finds support the theory that it dates from before 1600BC. The nearby **Museo di Torralba** displays excavated item from the nuraghe.

The final historical stop on this highway tour dates from the 12th century – a period which seems almost recent, compared with the Nuraghi culture. The site lies 20km (12 miles) outside Sassari, east off the SS131. At the exit for **Ploaghe** take the SS597, which ends in Olbia. From here you can see your destination, the **Chiesa di Santa Trinità di Saccargia** (open daily). The symmetrical black-and-white-striped church tower, built of basalt and limestone in Romanesque style, rises out of the landscape and it is not difficult to recognise the signature of the 12th-century Pisan artists. The 'Church of the Piebald Cow' was one of the churches intended to demonstrate the primacy of the Pisans. They built it on the site of an existing church and transferred their order here. The only extant cycle of 13th-century frescoes in Sardinia is located in the apse of the church, ascribed to an unknown Pisan master. Some 3km (2 miles) away stands another Romanesque church, the Chiesa di San Michele di Salvènero, also from the 12th century, but more traditional in style.

Nuraghi fortifications at Su Antine

Through the Wilds of Barbagia

A full day from Cagliari en route to Sassari: off the superstrada through the highlands of interior Sardinia, visiting villages famous for carnival, wine, lace and local crafts.

The Superstrada Carlo Felice, which links the cities of Cagliari and Sassari, is fast and comfortable, but a more scenic route is covered by the following tour, which takes one day by car. It leads directly through the mountains of interior Sardinia, a notorious and disreputable area in which banditry and vendettas were part of everyday life well into the second half of the last century.

Your point of departure is the exit from the SS131 by Villasanta, which leads directly to **Castello Las Plassas** and the Nuragic settlement of **Su Nuraxi** *(see page 37)*. Follow this road until you reach the first spurs of the Marmilla then slow down for the gentle curves up into the highlands where breathtaking views of the valley open up. After a few kilometres, you will arrive at the **Giara di Gesturi**, a basalt plateau of roughly 50 sq. km (19 sq. miles) which, because of its especially well protected location, was densely inhabited even in ancient times. As a result, you will find *nuraghi* executed in a wide variety of styles, among them the *Bruncu 'e Madugui*, believed to be the oldest fortress structure on Sardinia.

The mountain village of Aritzo

Twilight in the highlands

From the village of **Gesturi,** a 5-km (3-mile) road leads across the plateau, densely forested with cork-oaks and *màcchia,* and particularly famous for the small wild horses which still roam freely here *(see page 37).* Now follow the SS197 in the direction of Fonni, and take the left-hand turning to Asuni to visit the **Castello Medusa**, the gateway to the Barbagia region. Known locally as the Land of the Brabaxana, this is a magical place, where myths and legends flourish.

You are are now slowly nearing the **Monti del Gennargentu** with its peaks, **La Marmora** (1,834m/6,017ft) and the **Bruncu Spina** (1,829m/6,000ft). In winter you will occasionally encounter skiers here, and while the pastures in the valley are in bloom, up here your progress may be slowed by glare off the ice and snowdrifts. In this beautiful remote region, **Tonara** is renowned all over Italy for the best honey nougat and **Desulo** for its lace and colourful folk costumes.

If you want to stay in the area of the **Barbagia Belvi** and ascend La Marmora on a clear day, then with a little bit of luck you will be able to enjoy a panoramic view of all of Sardinia. For this purpose, **Aritzo** – which you will have passed just before Desulo – is the best starting-point.

Fonni, 25km (16 miles) from Desulo is, at 1,000m (3,280ft), the highest community on Sardinia and a popular meeting point for skiers. Several ski lifts lead to the summit of **Monte Spada**. In Fonni, the route divides, and you have a choice of how to continue. One option is to proceed to the SS131 through **Gavoi** and **Ollolai**. On the way it is worth a side trip to see the **Chiesa di Nostra Signora di Gonari**, one of the most im-

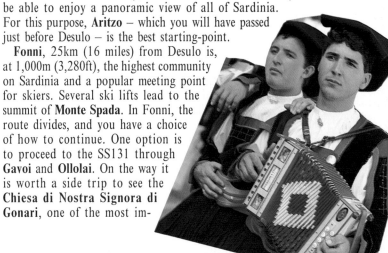

In the mountains between Oliena and Orgosolo

portant pilgrimage destinations in all of Sardinia. The road turns east at **Sarule**. The village of **Mamoiada** is famous for the wooden masks worn by the Mamuthones during the famous carnival procession that takes place on Shrove Tuesday. Nearby **Orgosolo** should not be missed: not only does it have excellent wine, but the village is covered in murals. The next main town is **Nuoro** with its excellent Museo della Vita e delle Tradizioni Sarde (closed Mon) and the Museo d'Arte di Nuoro (open Tues–Sun). From here, continue to **Orune**, with its beautiful view of the white cliffs of the **Monte Albo** and the sacred spring of **Su Tempiesu**. Further north, the route passes through the gigantic, almost deserted cork-oak forests around the village of **Bitti**. A large nuraghic village called **Romanzesu** has recently been discovered on the granite plateau surrounding the village.

The SS389 now leads on through the **Altopiano Buddoso** to **Pattada**. If you are interested in buying a beautiful hand-made shepherd's knife, you should stop here. **Ozieri** is known to visitors first and foremost as a site of great archaeological significance, and has lent its name to the prehistoric Ozieri Culture. Evidence that this former provincial capital was once a busy feudal centre is borne out by the magnificent classical buildings with their richly ornamented façades. Ozieri is a wealthy area today since, along with Macomer, it is the centre of Sardinian livestock breeding. Interesting sites are the Museo Archeologico, which houses finds from periods as early as 4500BC, and the Duomo, with its seven-sectioned retablo by the 'Master of Ozieri'. This artist – in whose work you can clearly see the mainland influence – is regarded, along with the 'Master of Castelsardo', as being one of the island's most significant. From Ozieri, it is only a few kilometres to the SS597, Sassari–Olbia highway.

Accommodation

Aritzo
SA MUVARA***
Via Funtana Rubia
Tel: 0784 629336;
fax: 629433
CASTELLO**
Corso Umberto 169
Tel/fax: 0784 629266
PARK HOTEL**
Via A. Maxia
Tel: 0784 629201; fax:
629318

Desulo
GENNARGENTU***
Via Kennedy
Tel/fax: 0784 619270
LA NUOVA*
Via Lamarmora
Tel: 0784 619251

Fonni
CUALBU***
Viale del Lavoro
Tel: 0784 57054; fax: 58403

Ozieri
MASTINO***
Via Vittorio Veneto 13
Tel: 079 787041

Tel: 0784 629336

Fonni
SU NINNIERI
Loc. Monte Spada
Tel: 0784 57729

Ozieri
RISTORANE ITALY
Corso Umberto 51
Tel: 0784 733035

Orgosolo
AI MONTI DEL GENNARGENTU
Loc. Settiles
Tel: 0784 402374

Sorgono
NUOVA MANDROLISAI
Near church of S. Mauro
Tel: 0784 60068

Restaurants

Aritzo
SA MUVARA

Nuraghe outside the village of Bitti

WEST COAST TOUR 7

A day-trip from Cagliari to Isola di Sant'Antioco and San Pietro, plus a visit to Carbónia and the necropolis at Monte Sirai.

With an area of 109 sq. km (42 sq. miles), the volcanic island of **Sant'Antioco** is the largest island off Sardinia, and the fourth largest in Italy. The main town was once one of the most significant cities in the entire western Mediterranean. The settlement, founded by the Phoenicians, was called Sulcis, and constituted an important trading centre, especially for the shipment of ores from the neigh-

On the ferry to San Pietro

bouring region of Iglesiente. Gradually, however, the island became depopulated as the result of Roman punitive measures and centuries of Arab raids. The **Museo Archeologico** (open daily) in the town has displays of recent excavations and archaeological finds. Today's islanders are descended from Ligurians freed from Arab rule who settled here. They have managed to preserve their own language and cuisine. The town of Sant'Antioco is reached from the Sardinian mainland via a causeway some 3km (2 miles) long which was initiated by the Carthaginians and completed by the Romans. Two pre-Nuragic menhirs, known locally as Su Papa

Costa Verde and
Isola S. Antioco

15 km / 9 miles

(The Priest) and Sa Mongia (The Nun) welcome you to the town. As you enter the town you will find signs to the **Tophet** (open daily), a ritual ground for the Phoenicians where their deceased children were cremated. The well-preserved urns and the **Necropolis** are fascinating. This is the oldest Phoenician settlement to be discovered in Sardinia, dating from the 9th century BC. You should also visit the **church of Sant'Antioco**, originally Byzantine, with a baroque façade, where the catacombs are open to the public.

Parallel streets and narrow houses shut off from the exterior world call up images of the Arab world in **Calasetta**, the island's second-largest town. Here, you will see little that seems strictly Sardinian, or even Italian. In the bar on the harbour you will still find the atmosphere unsullied by tourism. In winter the place is a period film set, with storms lashing the quay outside and old fishermen playing cards behind the frosty panes.

The town, with its picturesque port, is watched over by a ruined fortress. A drive around the sparsely populated island is not absolutely necessary, but you might make a rewarding little side trip to the old **tonnara**, or tuna cannery, located just a few kilometres outside the town. Schools of tuna swarm through the straits between San Pietro and Sant'Antioco every year, when they are caught by the thousands in nets. The *matanza*, or tuna hunt, is a bloody bit of theatre which attracts a large audience each May. A ferry departs almost hourly from Calasetta through the Canale delle Colonne for the neighbouring **Isola di San Pietro**.

Fortifications in Calasetta

The main village, **Carloforte**, is named after Carlo Emanuele III, king of Piedmont-Savoy, whose statue stands in the main square. The coastal boulevard as well as the façades of the houses are anything but Sardinian. This former Ligurian colony successfully defended itself against foreign influences and preserved its own way of life. The entire island resembles a little paradise. Villas and country houses are surrounded by pine forests, vineyards and blossoming bougainvillea bushes. The countless fishing boats in the harbour of Carloforte, the huge saltworks at the east end of town, as well as the agriculture in the interior all speak of the island's prosperity. The steep coastline with columns of trachyte at the **Punta delle Colonne** on the southern end of the island is particularly impressive, and is home to numerous species of birds. Conservationists are lobbying to have this region declared a national park. A trip to the bizarre **Capo Sandalo** in the western part of the island is equally rewarding. The **Guárdia dei Mori** (Carrot Guard) which rises as high as 211m (692ft) is, unfortunately, not accessible by car. The **tonnara** on the northern tip, **La Punta**, is also of considerable size and still in service.

The Ligurian tradition, and a touch of its Arab past, have been preserved in the cuisine of both these islands. The much acclaimed *casca* is a sort of Sardinian couscous with vegetables. *Pesto carlofortino* is basically a *pesto genovese* made of basil, pine nuts, parmesan cheese, garlic, salt, black pepper and olive oil, with the addition of tomatoes. Other Ligurian-Sardinian-Arabic specialities worth sampling are freshly caught *tonno* (tuna) and *pesce spada* (swordfish), both of which are best when grilled.

Returning to the mainland via the ferry at Portovesme, you now have a chance to visit the town of **Carbónia**. A few kilometres beyond the red and white striped towers of the surrounding refineries, you will reach the city known primarily for its Phoenician/Carthaginian ruins on the nearby **Monte Sirai** (archeological site open Tues–Sun). Once up there you can examine an acropolis and a large necropolis. Excavations have revealed that this was a Phoenician outpost settled by residents of Sulcis – the earlier name of today's Sant'Antioco – who first destroyed a Nuraghi fortress on the site and ousted the locally established population from the coasts, forcing them inland. The reason for this forceful takeover was the rich ore deposits located in the Iglesiente area, and important to the area's economy to this day. The Phoenician occupation was short-lived: soon afterwards, their own centre was taken over again by the Nuraghi.

The other interesting thing about Carbónia is that it was a planned city, founded by Benito Mussolini in the late 1930s. The dream of a self-sufficient Italy – achieving independent energy through the use of Sulcis coal – has never quite died in Carbónia, but still remains no more than a dream. Because of the coal's high sulphur content it is scarcely usable. But Carbónia has tried to hold its ground in the face of economic reality, striving to shed its image as a fascist-era coal town. The neoclassical architecture of the Piazza Roma, the *municipio* and the entire layout of the city give an impression of architectural hyperbole, transporting the visitor back to the days of *Il Duce*.

If you are spending a night in the Sulcis/Iglesiente area you should make an excursion to Siliqua (take the SS58). Here you can visit the **Castello di Acquafredda** where, according to Dante's *Inferno*, Count Ugolino died.

Accommodation

An overnight stay in the town of Sant'Antioco is not very interesting, so most of the hotels we mention in the following list are in Calasetta, in the more tourist-orientated area of the island. Most attractive, however, is the seclusion of San Pietro, where you are almost guaranteed a relaxing stay, so we include several Carloforte hotels. As in the rest of Sardinia, it is a good idea to reserve in advance by phone, especially in high season, and also in winter, when many hotels close.

Sant'Antioco
L'EDEN ✯✯✯
Piazza Parrocchia 15
Tel: 840768; fax 840769
MODERNO ✯✯
Via Nazionale 82
Tel: 83105; fax: 840252

Calasetta
HOTEL CALA DI SETA ✯✯✯
Via R. Margherita 61
Tel: 88304; fax: 31538
www.caladiseta.go.to
STELLA DEL SUD ✯✯✯
Loc. Spiaggia Grande
Tel: 810188; fax: 810148
www.hotelstelladelsud.com
FJBY ✯✯
Via Solferino 83
Tel: 88444; fax: 887089
www.emmeti.it

San Pietro – Carloforte
HIERACON ✯✯✯
Corso Cavour 63
Tel: 854028; fax: 854893
www.hotelhieracon.cjb.net
RIVIERA ✯✯✯
Corso Battellieri 26
Tel: 854004; fax: 856562
PAOLA ✯✯
Tacca Rossa
Tel: 850098
www.carloforte.net/hotelpaola

Restaurants
The hotels mentioned above have their own restaurants which are, for the most part, worth recommending. The restaurants listed below are pleasant alternatives. The **Da Nicola** in Carloforte and the **Tanit** in Carbónia are especially recommended for lunch as well as dinner. In addition,

Da Nicola serves Ligurian-Sardinian-Arabic specialities. Check the menu for *casca* (Sardinian couscous), *pesto carlofortino* (a special *pesto genovese*), *tonno* (tuna) and *pesce spada* (swordfish).

Sant'Antioco
LA LAGUNA
Lungomare A. Vespucci 37
Sant'Antioco
Tel: 83286
DA PASQUINO
Via Roma 99
Tel: 88473

San Pietro – Carloforte
AL TONNO DI CORSA
Via Marconi 47
Tel: 855106
DA NICOLO
Corso Cavour 32
Tel: 854048
VITTORIO
Corso Battellieri 11
Tel: 855200

Carbónia
TANIT
Loc. Sirai
Tel: 76393

Nuxis
LETIZIA
Via S.Pietro 10
Tel: 957021

What to Do
You can rent a boat in Calasetta and Carloforte, take a walk on the beaches, or drink a Campari in the harbour bar. There is little to buy here, but in the Cantina Social in Calasetta you can sample and purchase local wine directly from the producer.

The West Coast: Grottoes, Mines and Dunes

Full day tour covering the old mining works of Iglesias, the Grotta San Giovanni, and on through the winding Fluminese to the Costa Verde; includes an outing to the sand dunes.

Between Oristano and Cagliari, in the regions of Sulcis and Iglisiente, the Sardinian landscape displays its diversity. Your point of departure for this long and demanding day trip is **Iglesias**, an old mining centre in the heart of the region of the same name. Those coming in from Cagliari on highway SS130 who set out early enough, can take a short side trip through the **Grotta San Giovanni** (open daily) at **Domusnóvas**. Approximately 1km (⅝ mile) road follows the course of a raging river through this limestone grotto and it is the shortest route into the sparsely settled region of **Fluminese** which lies beyond it. At the end of the tunnel is a restaurant, bar and picnic area.

The landscape on the road to the city of Iglesias has been ravaged by centuries of mining zinc, silver and other ores. Continue straight on into the centre, because here you'll find beautiful old houses with artfully ornamented wrought-iron balconies. You will notice that this 13th-century town is radically different from the many unattractive and utilitarian miners' villages in Iglesiente. Under the rule of the Pisans, Iglesias was granted the right to

The ruins of Tharros

mint its own coins. Particularly during the evening *passegiatta,* which one sees in the **Piazza Municipio** in the heart of the old quarter, the city seems to reflect a brighter and less arduous era. The showpiece of the old quarter is the **Chiesa di Santa Chiara** (closed Thur), among the best Romanesque-Gothic structures on the island. Also located on the *piazza* is the **Ristorante Villa di Chiesa** which serves good Italian fare. In the **Museo Mineralogico** (open by appointment, tel: 0781 22304) are over 8,000 rare minerals and fossils as well as archaeological finds unearthed during mining work in the Iglesiente area.

The drive through the Iglesiente and Fluminese region requires a certain skill behind the wheel. If you take the road to Gonnesa then continue driving towards the sea you will come upon a splendid panorama. The **Pan di Zucchero** (Sugar Loaf) is a massive white rock just off the coast at **Masua**, and the drive between the old mining villages of Masua and Buggerru is unforgettable. The coastal road is very narrow and the bends make it an uncomfortable ride, but it is worth the trouble.

As an alternative, if you did not take the coastal road, follow the SS126 and look out for signs for the turning to the ruins of the **Tempio di Antas**, dedicated to the *Sardus pater,* the mythical original father of the Sardinians. Dating from the Carthaginian period, this holy place set in a dense oak forest was later taken over by the Romans. At the temple, a third of your route is behind you. Back on the SS126, you will see signs to the **Grotte Su Mannau** which has 6km (4 miles) of caves covered with stalactites and stalagmites. The next town north is **Fluminimaggiore** where you can visit the Antico Mulino Licheri ethnographic museum, which displays local artefacts and an ancient water mill.

Continue on the SS126 past **Arbus** and **Guspini**, which are about 25km (16 miles) from Fluminimaggiore, along a particularly winding stretch of road. Around 10km (6 miles) outside Arbus, at the Casa Atzeni, a side street branches off towards the old mining

In the dunes near Torre dei Corsari

area surrounding the village of **Ingurtosu**. This ghost village is abandoned but the manager's villa is worth a look.

The wonderful beach of **Piscina** is 9km (6 miles) from Ingurtosu; the dunes here cover about 30 sq. km (12 sq. miles). A protected area of 100-metre (330-ft) high dunes of fine sand are continually reshaped by the strong sea breeze and are home to various forms of wildlife. From **Guspini**, continue on the SS126 for about 25km (16 miles), passing the precipitous Monte Arcuento and the Montevecchio massif and then through fertile pasture lands until you arrive at the renowned sand dunes of the **Costa Verde**. The name refers to the *macchia* hinterland rather than the coastal margin itself, for its massive sand dunes have little in common with the greenness associated with its title.

From the holiday homes of **Marina di Arbus** a road first paved in 1989 follows the coast. By the time you reach **Torre dei Corsari** and **Porto Palma**, you will probably be breaking out a second roll of film, the dunes are so exquisitely beautiful. It is possible to horse ride through the dunes but during high season you must apply at least two weeks in advance at the **Hotel Ala Birdi** (tel: 0783 800268), a renowned equestrian centre which specialises in excursions, or alternatively in the village of Torre del Corsari. For non-riders, it is worth stopping here for a stroll along the beach or a swim. The further you get from the paved road, the more inviting the landscape becomes. Those who want to stay overnight on the Costa Verde will have a tough time, however, since most of the lodgings here are holiday cottages. If, despite this, you are still set on finding accommodation, you will get the best information in the local bars.

After an ardous series of bends you will arrive at the Golfo di Oristano, with the Stagno di Marceddi and the Stagno di San Giovanni situated behind. After rejoining the SS126, the next town along the route is **Arborea**. Attractions here include liberty and neo-gothic architecture and a town hall (closed Sat and Sun) with its collection of local Punic and Roman archeological finds. Those who do not want to stay overnight in Arborea, so named during the fascist period, should drive straight on to Oristano. Spend the night in **Oristano**, and the next morning you can make a side trip to the ancient city of Tharros. Oristano is the provincial capital, but not a very exciting town. It does have a Duomo (open daily), built in a mixture of architectural styles, and in the main square, the Piazza Eleonora, surrounded by lions, is a statue of Eleonora, the 14th-century *giudice* who published the *Carta di Logu*, a book on common law. The pedestrianised area in the historical centre has some new, elegant shops.

The site of the Carthaginian settlement of **Tharros** (open–dusk; admission charge) located on the Sinis Peninsula in the Golfo di Oristano area, is unique. Excavations here have brought to light paved streets, public baths, the houses of the city nobles, and even the former sewage system. A treasure trove of jewellery, pottery and glassware excavated here can be seen in the archaeological museums of Cagliari and Oristano. While you are here, it is delightful to take a morning swim beneath the ruins of the city in the protected waters of the gulf.

A few thatch-covered roofs of the fishermen's houses around the pilgrimage church of **San Giovanni di Sinis**, located several hundred metres from Tharros, are still representative of much of old Sardinia. The one-man boats, still made out of reed grass, could easily date from biblical times. The ancient church itself is interesting: it was originally a 6th-century place of worship, extended during the 13th century, using blocks of stone brought from Tharros.

A Fistful of Dollars is the association that comes to mind when you turn off into the tiny pilgrimage village of **San Salvatore** (open July–Aug, Tues–Thur). This place served as the backdrop for a series of 'spaghetti westerns' in the 1960s after the director Sergio Leone, among others, used the location as a cost-effective substitute for the Wild West.

The former **Nuragic water temple**, which you can explore while you are here, is today (like so many of the Nuragic holy places) a place of Christian pilgrimage, with accompanying pilgrims' cottages, known as *cumbessias*. This church is the focus of the annual nine-day parish festival in September, the Festival of the Redeemer, when the statue of Christ (San Salvatore) is carried here from Cabras by white-clothed young men, running barefoot.

Typical residences in Iglesias

Alghero: Bastion of Catalonia

A day tour of Alghero; a walk through the old quarter; an afternoon boat trip to Capo Cáccia and the Grotta di Nettuno.

Anyone who speaks Catalan but not Italian will do outstandingly well in **Alghero**. Its centuries-long connection with the Spanish mainland has been retained to the present day, and many residents of the city consider themselves more Spanish than Italian. Alghero was founded at the beginning of the 12th century and for 250 years was ruled by the Doria dynasty of Genoa, until they were forced to hand it over to the rulers of Aragon in 1353. This brought the first Catalan settlers to the city: they drove out the local Sardinians and Italians, and transformed Alghero into a bastion in the service of the Spanish Crown. These events left their stamp on every facet of Alghero's life. Even the streets here have two names: Prassa del Pou Vel and Carrer de Bonaire as well as **Piazza Civica** and **Via Umberto**.

A stroll through Alghero is best begun on the harbour front. Until a few decades ago fishing boats predominated, but today there are quite a few luxury yachts belonging to people for whom the yacht basin of Porto Cervo is too expensive for long-term mooring. The city walls have been left fully intact towards the open sea, so that this little community, surrounded by water on

The coast at Capo Cáccia

three sides, is well protected. A late afternoon stroll along the walls will take you to the **Lungomare Dante**, the seaside promenade, and the **Torre di Sperone**.

More than any other Sardinian city, this spa town has developed into a centre of tourism, propped up by its image as a 'coral city'. The selection of souvenirs on sale ranges from the kitsch to creative local work, but as many coral reefs around the world, including the local reefs, are being depleted, the buying of coral products should be strongly discouraged. A stroll through the old quarter need not follow any special route: you can just take off in any direction and find something interesting.

The churches are all thoroughly unusual and of particular beauty. The 14th-century monastery of **San Francisco,** considered the

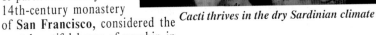
Cacti thrives in the dry Sardinian climate

most beautiful house of worship in the city, is somewhat hidden away in the **Carrer Major**, but the **Cattedrale di Santa Maria** (open daily 6.30am–noon; 5–8pm) and the baroque **Chiesa di San Michele** with its multicoloured dome, are easy to find.

L'Alguer – the Spanish name for the city – is a culinary high point of any trip to Sardinia. In contrast to the hearty Sardinian shepherds' dishes, fish – particularly lobster – takes pride of place here. The widely known 'lobster Catalan', already shelled, is available at most restaurants. You may also recognise *paella* from the Spanish mainland, fried sea anemone and *spaghetti bottariga* – pasta with fish. You can drink a fresh white *vermentino* from the nearby Fattoria di Santa Maria di Las Palmas, or an *arogosta* or *cala viola* from the Azienda Sella & Mosca.

The **Mercato** in the **Via Sassari** looks particularly inviting. Lobsters and other shellfish from the 'lobster coast' are displayed here on ice in large wooden boxes, alongside eel, squid and fresh

Hotel Villa Las Tronas

sea urchins. If you prefer to see your fish alive, the town also has a small aquarium just off the piazza.

Your afternoon could be devoted to a boat trip to one of the most renowned caves on Sardinia, the **Grotta di Nettuno** on Capo Cáccia (open summer 9am–7pm, winter 9am–2pm; entrance fee). The stunning view of the 200-m (655-ft) rock-falls on the cape should be compensation for the rather steep price of tickets. The boat ride takes 30 minutes and departs at 9 and 10am in the summer and 3 and 4pm in April, May and October. The Grotta di Nettuno is considered one of the most breathtaking stalactite caves on the island. The **Grotta dei Ricami** and the **Grotta Verde** are also worth a visit. They are accessible by boat and also via the SS127, but if you drive there's a long descent via a 600-step stone staircase after leaving your car.

This part of the excursion could be extended, finishing up with a swim at the **Cala di Calciano** or the **Porto Conte**. This side trip also takes you past **Fertilia**, a city founded by settlers from the Po River Delta during Mussolini's rule. Between Alghero and Fertilia is the **Stagno di Calich**, and between Fertilia and Porte Conte, you will pass the **Palmavera Nuraghe** (open daily, guided tours available), the main tower of which dates from the 14th century BC. This *nuraghe* is a fortified complex with an interior courtyard to which access was particularly difficult. A village surrounded the defensive tower, and the foundation walls of the residential section are still visible.

Alghero is best suited as a base camp for a stay of several days, during which you can make excursions into the surrounding areas. The majority of the hotels are located a short distance outside of the city centre on the **Spiagga di San Giovanni**, on and around the **Via Lido** in Fertilia, and some on the **Porto Conte** (some 10km/6 miles away) and the **Torre Nuova**. There you have the advantage of quieter – but not cheaper – accommodation and, if you are lucky, a view of the sea and the romantic sunsets over Capo Cáccia. The best address in Alghero is the **Hotel Villa Las Tronas**, situated on a little peninsula beyond the city. This former holiday 'cottage' of the Italian kings today functions as a first-class hotel and has managed to create a successful combination of nostalgic ambience and modern luxury. Another good choice is the **Hotel San Francesco**, in a convent attached to the San Francesco monastry with clean simple rooms.

Unlike most of Sardinia's cities, there are a number of good bars and pubs in Alghero. If you visit Alghero at Easter you will see the *Settimana Santa* (*La Setmana Santa a L'Alquer* in Catalan), which is one of the most beautiful processions in all Sardinia. Its high point is reached with Christ's descent from the cross, solemnised in the Cathedral, followed by a lengthy procession of lights which wends its way through the old quarter, where devout women cover their faces with black Spanish lace *mantillas*. These Easter celebrations are something to remember, but don't forget that many hotels get fully booked well in advance.

Accommodation

Alghero is a good base for a stay of several days. There are many amenities in the city, which is well equipped to handle tourists, and the surrounding area is extremely inviting, especially the picturesque scenery of Capo Cáccia. Many interesting sights are within reach of Alghero, so there is no reason to settle in noisy Sassari, for example, since Alghero is only half an hour away by car. Furthermore, Alghero is considered by many the culinary capital of Sardinia, noted for its fresh lobster and excellent wines. Finally, it possesses by far the widest selection of accommodation to be found on the island.

Annual Easter procession

Alghero
(Dialling Code 079)

CARLOS V★★★★
Lungomare Valencia 24
Tel: 979501; fax: 980298
www.hotelcarlosv.it

HOTEL CATALUNYA★★★★
Via Catalogna 24
Tel: 953172; fax: 953177
www.hotelcatalunya.it

VILLA LAS TRONAS★★★★
Lungomare Valencia 1
Tel: 981818; fax: 981044

LA PLAYA★★★
Via Pantelleria 14
Tel: 950369; fax: 985713

HOTEL SAN FRANCESCO★★
Via Ambrogio Machin 2
Tel/fax: 980330;
E-mail: hotsfran@tin.it

Alghero – Fertilia
DEI PINI★★★★
Loc. Le Bombarde
Tel: 930157; fax: 930259
www.hoteldeipini.it

BELLAVISTA★★★
Lungomare Rovigno 13
Tel: 930190; fax: 930124;
E-mail: bellavistafertilia@
tiscali.it

HOTEL FERTILIA★★
S. Statale S. Maria la Palma
Tel: 930098; fax: 930522

Porte Conte
CAPO CACCIA★★★★
Loc. Capo Caccia
Tel: 946666; fax: 946535
www.hotelcapocaccia.it

PORTO CONTE★★★★
Baia di Conte
Tel: 942035; fax: 942045
www.hotelportoconte.com

EL FARO★★★★
Porto Conte
Tel: 942010; fax: 942030
www.elfarohotel.it

Restaurants
Alghero is a gourmet's paradise, with a number of great restaurants. Fish dishes and dishes with a Spanish influence characterise the cuisine. The food is complemented by the best white wine on Sardinia – the *terre bianche* from the cellars of Sella and Mosca, and the *vermentino* from the Cantina Sociale Riforma in S. Maria La Palma. There is no contest: the best restaurant in town is La Lepanto.

AL TUGURI
Via Maiorca 113
Tel: 976772

LA LEPANTO
Via Carlo Alberto
Tel: 979116

LA MURAGLIA
Bastioni Marco Polo
Tel: 975577

PALAU REAL
Via S. Erasmo
Tel: 980688

PAVONE
Piazza Sulis 3/4
Tel: 979584

What to Do
Your best bet is to wander through the old quarter, stopping for a cold beer or tall drink at a local bar. Don't expect very sophisticated establishments, but even in Porto Conte, you will find discos and, in summer, a flourishing beach nightlife.

A Day's Outing to Bosa

A drive down the lobster coast; a stroll through historic Bosa on the River Temo; the Bosa Marina; wine tasting; plus dinner.

The route out of Alghero follows a coastal road built only a few years ago, which provides a fascinating view of the so-called 'lobster coast'. There are cliffs several hundred metres high here, with sheer drops extending for some 45km (28 miles). This region is one of the last refuges of the **griffon vulture**, whose existence on Sardinia is seriously threatened by the progressive opening up of the coastal areas.

Half way to Bosa get on the SS292 for an interesting inland excursion. **Villanova Monteleone** is an ancient farming community renowned for traditional carpets made of untreated wool, woven in geometric designs. Just before entering the village you come across the **Fontana del Paradiso** (Paradise Fountain), known for its fresh, slightly sweet water. According to tradition the water protects against sadness and misfortune. If you have time, continue on this road towards Torralba, to visit one of the largest *nuraghi* in Sardinia, known as the Nuraghe S. Antine *(see page 38)*.

Back on the coast road, where the scenery is truly beautiful, continue towards the old port city of **Bosa**, which is otherwise only accessible via the tortuous and twisting roads from Cagliari and Macomer. The road enters Bosa near the mouth of the **Temo** – the only river on Sardinia navigable by ship. However, it is worth your while to drive on a bit further towards **Suni**; from the

View over the roofs of Bosa

Fishing boats moored on the Temo

hairpin bends of the road you will get beautiful views of the picturesque medieval city, lorded over by the fortress of the **Castello Malaspina** (open daily 10am–noon, 4–7pm). This stronghold of the Genoan Malaspina family was erected in 1112, and shelters in its chapel an interesting fresco cycle dating from the 14th and 15th centuries.

A stroll through the narrow alleyways of the old city of Bosa transports you into centuries past. Entering from the **Corso Vittorio Emanuele II** and passing the **Chiesa del Carmine** and the **Cattedrale** (closed noon–4pm), you arrive, by way of the historic **Temo Bridge**, the old **Sas Concas** tannery houses with their pointed roofs. Looking out from the little square at the river's edge, you have a splendid view of the town, with its very un-Sardinian atmosphere. The palm-fringed river promenade passes stately façades, dating from the time when Bosa was still the provincial capital.

Across the river, pitching and tossing in the river are the old sailboats of the fishermen, who bring their catch up here from the sea. At the northern bridgehead, the last representatives of the basket weavers' guild continue their work. The women of the town offer their handmade lace and net-work for sale in the weathered, musty entrances to their houses.

From the southern bridgehead, a small road leads some 2km (1¼ miles) upwards from the Temo to the beautifully situated church of **San Pietro**, begun in 1072. The path leads through fertile gardens, orchards and groves of orange trees and palms, and there are wonderful views when you arrive. The **Bosa Marina**, with its long road along the shore and mouth of the river, is equally worth a little side trip, particularly if you follow the road yet further on – up to Magomadas and the chapel of **Santa Maria del Mare**, where

The Malaspina stronghold

a lovely view of the coast opens up. The vineyards of **Malvasia di Bosa** are also located here. They produce *malvasia*, a dry dessert wine which resembles sherry. Even if it cannot quite compare with the finest of the southern wines, such as those from Lipari, it is nonetheless a special treat. You can buy it in many shops in Bosa, or get it directly from the vintners or at their trade association, the Cooperativa Cantina Sociale in **Flussio**, which produces an extraordinarily strong *malvasia*.

In Bosa, the **Da Tattore** on the Piazza Monumento is a simple, well-managed restaurant that serves outstanding fish dishes and a delicious white house wine.

Accommodation

(Dialling Code 0785)

AL GABBIANO✩✩✩
Viale Mediterraneo
Tel/fax: 374123

MANNU HOTEL✩✩✩
Via Alghero
Tel: 375306; fax: 375308

PERRY CLAN✩✩✩
Via Alghero
Tel: 373074; fax: 375263

COSTA CORALLO✩✩
Via Colombo 11/13
Tel: 375162; fax: 375529

MIRAMARE✩
Via Colombo
Tel: 373400

Restaurants

BORGO S IGNAZIO
Via S Ignazio 33
Tel: 374662

DA TATTORE
Piazza Monumento
Tel: 373104

NIEDDU
Via Genova
Tel: 373157

Alghero to Sassari via Porto Torres

A trip north from Alghero to Sassari; a wine-tasting stop en route at the vineyards of Sella & Mosca; Ozieri ruins at Anghelu Ruju; and optional detour to historic Porto Torres with its Roman and Romanesque sites.

Leaving Alghero on the SS291, you must initially fight your way through the traffic endemic in this little city. Petrol stations and small businesses line your route, encouraging you to hurry along as fast as possible in the direction of the airport, which is located about 10km (6 miles) out of town on the SS291. Soon after the turn off for the *aeroporto,* a large sign for Sella & Mosca heralds a worthwhile stop. Turn right into Sardinia's largest vineyard and winery and head for the **Sella & Mosca Wine Museum** (open daily, visits to the cellars by appointment Mon–Fri 5.30–6.30pm, Sat during the summer, tel: 079 997700).

Sella & Mosca are among the best-known Sardinian vintners and hold their own against overpowering competition from Tuscany and the Piedmont. Their best-known wine is the *Anghelu Ruju*

The necropolis at Anghelu Ruju

Alghero and Sassari

15 km / 9 miles

Itinerary 9
Itinerary 10
Itinerary 11

(named after the necropolis located on the other side of the road). This is a strong, well-rounded dessert wine with the designation *riserva*, an assurance of outstanding maturity and excellence. This *riserva*, which reaches an alcohol content of up to 18 percent, is fermented using Cannonau grapes, and is served at a temperature of between 12–14°C (54–57°F). Revelling in the delights of a 1979 *Anghelu Ruju* is a very good way to round off a stay on Sardinia. The *Tanca Farra*, a dry red wine containing 12.5 percent alcohol, is produced from Cannonau and Cabernet Sauvignon grapes.

You should also sample the white *vermentino Cala Viola*, a light wine with a refreshing taste that harmonises nicely with fish dishes. The *Terre Bianche* is a real speciality. This white wine is fermented from Torbato grapes. It is a dry wine of the highest quality which is recommended as an accompaniment for both fish and meat courses.

Located across the way from the *fattoria* – hidden inconspicuously behind a wire fence – are the *domus de janas* of **Anghelu Ruju** (open Oct–Feb 9.30am–4pm; Mar–Sept 9am–7pm). The ruins are from the Ozieri Culture dating from the late neolithic period (3500BC) but were used until 1800BC. They are believed to be burial vaults, imitations of the dwellings of the period, built on a smaller scale to house the dead and their belongings to ensure comfort in the next life.

At the sharp bend in the SS291, you must decide whether you want to drive directly on to Sassari (approximately 20km (12 miles) or whether you would perhaps prefer to take a 60-km (36-mile) detour through the sparsely settled region of **Nurra** towards **Porto Torres** on the Golfo dell'Asinara. On the SS131 just before Porto Torres, at km 222.3, there is something you should not miss. The pre-nuragic sanctuary of **Monte d'Accoddi** (open daily; summer guided tours 9am–6pm) is an example unique in Sardinia (and the whole of the western Mediterranean) of a megalithic altar, where rituals and sacrifices were celebrated to ensure the fecundity of the earth. The site dates from 4500BC.

Six km (4 miles) further along is **Porto Torres**. The island's first Roman city, known as Turris Libisonis, was founded in 27BC, and became well known in ancient Rome because its inhabitants were already carrying on a thriving trade with the mainland. As often happens on Sardinia, the whole city is not very impressive, but there are a handful of attractions which make a visit worthwhile.

The **Antiquarium Turritano** (Archaeological Museum; Via Ponte Romano; open daily Tues–Sat, Sun 9am–1.20pm) houses all the findings from the ancient Turris Libisonis and is well worth your time. Also worth a look are the **Terme Centrali** (Thermal Baths), which date from the 3rd–4th century BC. The **Basilica di San Gavino** (open 7am–noon and 4–7.30pm), in the old town, was finished in 1111, and became the burial place of the martyr St Gavin. It is among the most significant Romanesque buildings on the island.

Due to the fact that Porto Torres is one of the most important harbours on Sardinia, in the summer thousands of holiday-bound visitors stream off the huge ferries of the state and privately operated lines.

From the town you have an excellent view of the Isola Asinara, which was formerly a high-security prison. The island is now a national park and it is possible to arrange guided tours of the island's wildlife (tel: 0337 756945). Asinara is famous for its wild white donkeys which give the island its name (*asino* means donkey in Italian).

Accommodation	Restaurants
(Dialling Code 079)	Porto Torres has one of the
ELISA☆☆☆	top 10 restaurants on Sardinia,
Via Mare 2	the Li Lioni, which also has a
Tel: 513260	garden.
LIBYSSONIS☆☆☆	DA ELISA
Loc. Serra dei Pozzi	Via Mare 2
Tel: 501613; fax: 501600	Tel: 513260
TORRES☆☆☆	LI LIONI
Via Sassari 75	SS131, Loc. Li Lioni
Tel: 501604; fax: 501605	Tel: 502286
ROYAL☆	SCOGLIO LUNGO
Via S. Satta 8	Lungomare Balai
Tel: 502278	Tel: 501300

VENDEMMIA
1988

S. Maria La Palma

Aragosta

VERMENTINO DI ALGHERO
VINO DA TAVOLA

IMBOTTIGLIATO ALL'ORIGINE DALE
CANTINA SOCIALE RIFORMA AGRARIA DI

S. Maria La Palma - Italia
750 ml ℮   PRODOTTO IN ITALIA

A Day in Sassari

A day in the city of Sassari, including a visit to the Museo Nazionale G. A. Sanna and a shopping stroll along the Corso Vittorio Emanuele.

With its rather unattractive outlying districts, its skyline of tall buildings, superhighway and shopping malls, **Sassari** at first appears to be some kind of urban blot. More reminiscent of the mainland in atmosphere, Sassari has a less provincial air than Cagliari, with which it has vied for centuries for the rank of first island city. It owes its big city character primarily to those well-to-do business families who built their ostentatious trade 'palaces' here during the Genoan-Pisan epoch. However, Sassari, the site of Sardinia's first university, has not staked its reputation purely on the basis of material well-being. This is the birthplace of such people as ex-President Francesco Cossiga and Enrico Berlinguer, one of the leading figures in European communism. The **Brigata Sassari**, a heroic World War I military brigade, is still a source of local pride and a monument has been erected here.

You should begin your tour through the city in the **Piazza**

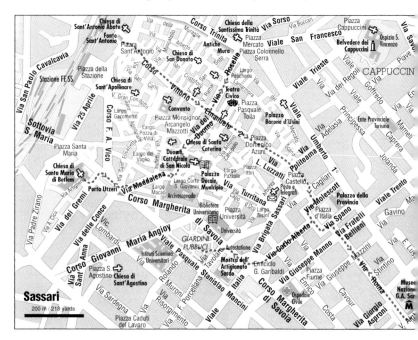

The Corso Vittorio Emanuele

Sant'Antonio below the central station. This is also the entrance to the **Corso Vittorio Emanuele** which, with its numerous shops, invites you to enjoy a bout of window shopping. The Corso is the stage for the two most important events in Sassari. In May, the **Cavalcata Sarda** (Cavalcade) takes place. The festival features a horse-back parade of riders in traditional costume who later take place in a horse race. Participants are drawn from surrounding villages and it is an excellent opportunity to see the folk costumes of the region. Over the weekend, folk groups perform traditional song and dance in the Piazza d'Italia during the evening. In August the town holds the spectacular **Candelieri** (Feast of Candles), when brightly costumed teams carry huge wooden candles in a dancing, pirouetting procession along the arches of the Corso.

This broad street with its twisted little side alleys, ends at the **Piazza Azuni**. From here you can see the pulsating heart of Sassari between the generously laid out **Piazza d'Italia** with its statue of Vittorio Emanuele, and the magnificent **Palazzo della Provincia**. Here, in front of the monument to the former king, half the local population seems to gather at sunset, providing the visitor with an insight into the Sardinian lifestyle, as they saunter about under the palms or besiege the cafés beneath the arcades.

The **Via Roma** leads from the heart of the old city into the modern outlying districts. After two intersections you reach the **Museo Archeologico Nazionale G.A. Sanna** (open Tues–Sun 9am–7.30pm; entrance fee) which, along with the Museo Archeologico in Cagliari, possesses the island's most significant collection of archaeological finds and folkloric materials, which are displayed only during temporary exhibitions. Seventeen galleries are dedicated to the various historical epochs – from the Neolithic period to the Nuraghi culture and on to the Phoenician age.

The Piazza d'Italia

If you are interested in Sardinian handicrafts, go back to the Piazza d'Italia and walk down Via Carlo Alberto through the Emiciclo Garibaldi to the **Giardini Pubblici**. Here, in the **Padiglione dell'Artigianato** (open Mon–Fri 9am–1pm), you will find a display of Sardinian crafts ranging from carpets to gold jewellery. Back on the Corso Emanuele you'll find the most popular street in the old town, the **Via al Rosello**, once a street of silversmiths, which today has few remaining craftsmen. This old city alley leads to the Fontana di Rosello (near the Chiesa della Santissima Trinità), the old source of drinking water, which still splashes out of the lions' jaws – although now only for aesthetic purposes. This is a real luxury on Sardinia, a dry island often plagued by water shortages. Today this beautiful fountain, ornamented with rose-coloured marble and endowed with four lions and seasonal allegories, is a bit off the beaten track. Where once the inhabitants of the city and travellers met, today there is no one. A large bridge now arcs over this beautiful place, elbowing the fountain out of the flow of the city and forming the quickest route to Sassari's public housing complex.

The churches of Sassari deserve a tour of their own. The heart of the city is the **Cattedrale** (open daily), with façades embellished in the Spanish style, their baroque excess making them look rather kitsch. Inside the cathedral, you should have a look at the painted processional standard which dates from the 15th century.

More significant in the estimation of the indigenous faithful, however, is the **Chiesa di Santa Maria di Betlem** (open daily), since the huge wooden processional candles used in the Candelieri festival are kept here all year round. Inside the cloisters is a 14th-century fountain which once supplied the town with water. From the cathedral, you can reach the church via the **Via Maddalena** or the city park by following the **Viale Coppino**.

Sassari is also worth a voyage of culinary exploration. Try your luck in any of the small restaurants in the narrow alleyways of the old quarter. Most of the dishes are simple but delicious. In some cases the bars are little more than remodelled living rooms, as you will find, for example, in the neighbourhood of the city hall. The only thing dangerous about **Da Tommaso** in the Via Ospizio Cappuccini is its nickname – **Trattoria L'Assassino**. At the end of the Corso on the Piazza Sant'Agostino, you will find the **Familiari**, which sometimes serves swordfish and tuna. The best restaurant in Sassari is the **Gianni e Amadeo**, also known as **Giamaranto**, in the Via Alghero. For your *primo* (first course) you could try *frutti di mare crudi* (mixed raw seafood) or *insalata di funghi porcini* (salad of wild mushrooms), along with Sardinian ham and *salciccia* (sausage). *Ravioli al carciofi* (ravioli with artichokes) is also recommended. Naturally, everything is home made. As a *secondo* (main course) try a *grigliata di pesce* (a dish of grilled fish) or an *insalata di aragosta* (lobster salad) along with the finest of Sardinian wines, perhaps a *Tanca Farra* or a *Vigne Pires di Tempio*. The winter cuisine in Sassari is more hearty and restaurants add bean soup or *giogga* (snails) to their menus.

Accommodation	Restaurants
(Dialling Code 079)	**CASTELLO** Piazza Castello 6
GRAZIA DELEDDA✩✩✩✩ Viale Dante 47 Tel: 271235; fax: 280884	Tel: 232041 **GIAMARANTO** Via Alghero 69
FRANK HOTEL✩✩✩✩ Via A. Diaz 20 Tel/fax: 276456	Tel: 274598 **FLORIAN** Via Capitano
LEONARDO DA VINCI✩✩✩ Via Roma 79 Tel: 280744; fax: 276456	Bellieni 27 Tel: 236251 **IL SENATO**
MARINI DUE✩✩✩ Via Pietro Nenni 2 Tel: 277282; fax: 280300	Via Gioacchino Mundula 2 Tel: 231423 **L'ASSASSINO**
GALLURA✩ Vico S. Leonardo 9 Tel: 238713	Vico Ospizio Cappuccini Tel: 235041 **TRE STELLE DA ANTIOCO**
SASSARI HOTEL✩ Via Umberto 65 Tel: 239543	Via Porcellana 6 Tel: 232431

From Sassari to Castelsardo

A day-long outing from Sassari to Castelsardo; plus a swim on the Platamona Lido, and dinner at the Ernesto; with an optional overnight stay in Castelsardo.

If you have a further day in Sassari at your disposal, you have time for this relaxing excursion which takes you via Sennori to the little village of **Castelsardo** (about an hour by car) on the SS200. The village is renowned for the quality of its lobster and mussels, as well as for the *Lunissanti* procession during Easter. Castelsardo, picturesquely situated atop a steep cliff, is overlooked by the Genoan castle to which the town owes its name. Castel Genovese, Castel Aragone, Castel Sardo: since the town was founded in 1102 it has changed titles as often as its occupants. However, it is known particularly as the home of the Maestro di Castelsardo, by far the most famous of Sardinia's 16th-century painters who, among his many works, produced the painting in

Saracen tower on the north coast

the **Cattedrale Sant'Antonio Abate**. With its enchanting old alleyways and picturesque location above the little harbour, Castelsardo is very attractive to tourists, and there is the usual proliferation of souvenirs. Despite the busloads of visitors, the town has managed to preserve much of its atmosphere and authenticity. Take a stroll through the cramped streets of the 'castle mountain', and pay a visit to the **Museo dell'Intreccio Mediterraneo** (open summer 9.30am–1pm, 3–7.30pm; winter 3–6pm). The musuem displays a collection of basketwork and weaving. If things prehistoric interest you, go a few kilometres outside Castelsardo,

View of Castelsardo

where, at the intersection with the road for Sedini, stand the famous **Roccia l'Elefante** (Elephant Rock). Hidden inside them are some *domus de janas*, relief-ornamented burial chambers dating from the time of the Ozieri Culture.

The afternoon could be devoted primarily to rest and relaxation in peaceful surroundings. First, the route leads back in the direction of Sassari, branching off, however, towards Porto Torres. Shady pine groves and sand dunes hide the expansive **Platamona Lido** and its offshoots, such as the **Marina di Sorso** with its water park. The town of Platamona has been the main playground for swimming enthusiasts from Sassari since its founding in the 1950s. Some of that fifties atmosphere still lives on: as far as the eye can see there are sun loungers and sun umbrellas, beach bars selling *granite* or Campari sodas, *gelati* sellers and pinball machines – the noise of radios creating a fitting audible background for this idyllic beach scene.

The Platamona Lido is by no means one of the private beaches so highly prized today. It offers instead the classic Italian beach scene in all its glory. If you can resist the pleasure of jumping into the water here, you may relax on the terrace of the **Ernesto**, a popular restaurant which serves outstanding fish specialities. If you don't feel like driving the 20km (12 miles) back to Sassari, go back to Castelsardo where you will find accommodation at the **Hotel Riviera** (Lungomare Anglona 1, tel: 079 470143), a hotel highly recommended for an overnight stay. The **Al Cormorano** restaurant (Via Cristoforo Colombo 5, tel: 079 669185) specialies in traditional Sardinian dishes and is one of the best places to eat in town. Castelsardo is also conveniently close to Valledoria and Costa Paradiso, a few kilometres further up the coast, if you feel like visiting them the following morning.

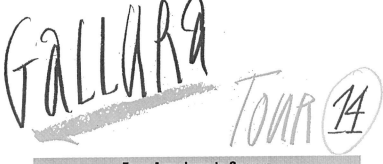

From Arzachena to Caprera

A round-trip tour of the north-eastern section of the island stopping in Santa Teresa di Gallura, Palau and the Capo d'Orso, with a brief visit to the islands of La Maddalena and Caprera, where the Casa Garibaldi can be visited.

As far as appearances go, at least when viewed from a distance, **Arzachena** might well be located in the Dolomites. It contrasts vividly with the granite walls of the surrounding mountains. For centuries, the region around Arzachena consisted of nothing more than farm and grazing land. Today, the area comprises a wealthy province whose coffers have been decidedly fattened by the tourism spilling over from the Costa Smeralda. The pronounced difference between this and the poorer regions of the Gennargentu is immediately striking.

The area around this pretty little town contains significant archaeological finds which merit an excursion in themselves. Especially impressive among these sites are the two *tombe di giganti* ('giants' graves') – of **Lu Coddu Vecchiu**, about 4.5km (3miles) from the town and **Li Lolghi** a few kilometres further on.

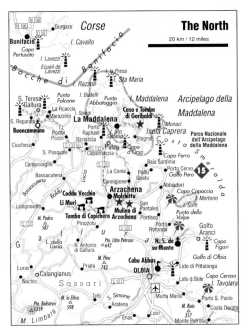

Leave town in the direction of Luogosanto and then follow the signs which guide you left to the first of the giants' graves. Lu Coddu Vecchiu, surrounded by a landscape of vineyards and gently rolling hills, is one of the most completely intact burial places on the island.

Its construction has been dated to around the 2nd millennium BC. Its central obelisk rises up 4m (13ft) and overlooks the entrance to the grave site. To the right and left of it, elevated

In the heart of Gallura: Arzachena

platforms create a semicircular plaza. Li Lolghi – very similar in layout to Coddu Vecchiu – is located a couple of kilometres away. Return to the main road and drive on further in the direction of Lougusanto. A sandy track leads off to the right of the town towards the nearby stone tombs of **Li Muri**, which date from the Neolithic age.

Lunch back in Arzachena is highly recommended, so that you can try the fresh fish at **La Zattera** (via Nazionale 35, tel: 0789 88235). Following an afternoon nap you might like to make a short excursion on the SS427 (a narrow road leading off the SS125). Just beside **Sant'Antonio di Gallura,** by an artificial lake, you'll see an ancient forest of wild olive trees which contains a giant olive tree, one of the oldest and largest in Europe; it is said that it takes 10 people to span its girth.

Just off the SS125 you will see signs for **Nuraghe Albucciu.** It is one of the rarer type of corridor *nuraghi*, which does not have the typical defensive central tower. Opposite the *nuraghe* is the start of the path to the **Temple Malchittu,** also part of the compound. A few kilometres further on you will reach the point where the road branches off towards **Palau** and **Baia Sardinia**, the most northerly points of the Costa Smeralda.

If you follow the road to Palau you will come to **Cannigione,** a pleasant little fishing village which has been transformed into a seaside town. Camp grounds and surfing schools border this stretch, which turns into a loose gravel road a few kilometres before Palau. After a short distance you will be able to see ahead of you the inlet of the Golfo di Saline, surrounded by gently ascending hills among which a holiday village is nestled.

Just behind it is the **Capo d'Orso** (Bear Cape), so-called because the weathered granite cliffs resemble a bear. This is yet another 'heraldic' image in the Sardinian gallery to stand alongside the elephants of Castelsardo and Costa Smeralda, and the mushroom rock of Arzachena. **Palau,** founded in the 18th century as a connecting port for the island of La Maddalena situated opposite, still lives today on proceeds derived from the ferry operation, which has in recent years become an extremely lucrative concern. The robust little ships ply back and forth from early in the morning until far into the night. Don't pass up the opportunity to take a boat ride and see the Capo d'Orso from the sea. Before undertaking this, however, a delicious lunch is recommended. At the **Da Franco** on the Via Capo d'Orso, you will find the hearty traditional fare of Gallura, such as the bread soup based on mutton broth which is called *zuppa cuata* as well as numerous excellent fish dishes which are a speciality.

Isola di La Maddalena, consisting in part of a closed-off NATO military zone, and **Isola Caprera** are well worth the short cruise. Both of these islands, which are today connected by a causeway, are part of the former land bridge which once linked Corsica and Sardinia. As a result of the shifting of the land masses, a small archipelago with more than 20 (mostly uninhabited) islands came into being.

The islands themselves really should be explored by boat. You will find many hidden delights, and there are places where boats are the only means of access. Excursions around the islands can be booked at the Consorzio degli Operatori Turistici dell'Arcipelago della Maddalena (tel: 0789 730071).

The only town of any size on Isola di La Maddalena is called

The picture book coast of Gallura

La Maddalena. It has a noble *palazzo* and some other elegant buildings, and is now somewhat in vogue. Also of interest is the **Museo Archeologico Navale Nino Lamboglia** (Maritime Museum, currently closed), which is dedicated to the Roman cargo ship found in the area.

On the island of Caprera, the **Compendio Garibaldi** (open winter Tues–Sat 9am–1.30pm, Sun 9am–noon, summer 9am–6.30pm) is a pilgrimage destination for Italian patriots from all over the

The 'Giants' Graves' at Lu Coddu Vecchiu

country – and perhaps for anyone who is interested in Italian unification and remembers Giuseppe Garibaldi as its hero and most romantic figure. It was to Caprera that he retreated during the years when he was barred from political office, piloting a small cutter and operating a trade in building materials between Nice (his home town) and Sardinia. After an odyssey which took him around the world, Garibaldi returned to this islet again in 1855 and, with a small inheritance, bought a portion of the island of Caprera. Some four years later he became heavily involved in politics once more, but he always missed Caprera when he was away, and it was here that he died, in 1882.

Back in Palau once more, take the SS133 which leads you through dense *màcchia* and bizarre rock formations to the most northerly community in Sardinia, **Santa Teresa di Gallura**. This little city, founded under Vittorio Emanuele I, is very popular today, primarily because of its numerous recreational opportunities. The bathing beach is perfect for both surfers and divers, and the bars and clubs provide lively nightlife. The Corsican port of Bonifacio is only 16km (10 miles) away. The main attraction in the surrounding area is the **Capo Testa**, another 5km (3 miles) from the city. Wind and rain have metamorphosed the granite here into impressive natural sculptures. Stone quarries were also once located here, and the building material for two columns of the Roman Pantheon as well as portions of the Leaning Tower of Pisa was quarried from the stone of Capo Testa.

For the return route to Arzachena you should take the SS133 once again and then continue via the SS125. Located on the latter road is **La Griglia** restaurant. In this former farmhouse, food is accompanied by freshly baked *carta da musica* or *pane carasau* (sheet of music) because the bread is baked in crisp flat circular loaves. Bread and mutton soup, *zuppa cuata*, is also on the menu and it is a good place to try the hearty and aromatic cooking which characterises the northern part of the island.

Accommodation

Arzachena provides an opportunity to be near, but not on, the Costa Smeralda, at a much lower cost. Prices in Cannigione are also significantly lower than those on the Baia Sardinia. On the eastern shore of the Golfo di Arzachena there is also the best campsite on Sardinia: Villaggio Isuledda Camping, tel/fax: 0789 86003.

Arzachena
(Dialling Code 0789)

HOTEL DELFINO☆☆☆
Viale Costa Smeralda
Tel: 83420; fax: 83542

CITTI☆☆
Viale Costa Smeralda 197
Tel: 82662; fax: 81920

Baia Sardinia
GRAND HOTEL SMERALDO
BEACH☆☆☆☆
Tel: 99046; fax: 99500

CORMORANO☆☆☆☆
Strada dei Pini
Tel: 99020; fax: 99290

MON REPOS HERMITAGE☆☆☆☆
Via Tre Monti
Tel: 99011; fax: 99050

LA BISACCIA☆☆☆
Tel: 99002; fax: 99162

DELLE VIGNE☆☆☆
Tel: 99860; fax: 99330

Cannigione
BAJA☆☆☆
Via Nazionale 35
Tel: 88010; fax: 88053

HOTEL DEL PORTO☆☆☆
Lungomare Andrea Doria
Tel: 88011; fax: 88064

LI CIPANNI☆☆☆
Loc. Li Cipanni
Tel: 86041; fax: 86200

STELLE MARINE☆☆☆
Loc. Mannena
Tel: 86305; fax: 86332

Restaurants

As well as the restaurants mentioned in the text – **Da Franco** and **La Griglia** – there is one of the top 10 restaurants on the island on Baia Sardinia, the **Grazia Deledda**, in addition to the excellent **Mistral** in La Maddalena.

DA FRANCO
Via Capo d'Orso 1
Palau
Tel: 709558

GRAZIA DELEDDA
Loc. Tiltizza
Baia Sardinia
Tel: 98988
(Closed 1 Nov–31 March)

LA GROTTA
Via Principe di Napoli 3
La Maddalena
Tel: 737228

LA QUERCIA DA ZIA PAOLINA
Via Tempo 7
Cannigione
Tel: 66075

LA GRIGLIA
Stazzu Pulcheddu – SS125
Tel: 708143

MISTRAL
Via Mazzini 2
La Maddalena
Tel: 738088

Costa Smeralda

A day on the Costa Smeralda: includes some beautiful swimming coves, plus tips on accommodation, dining and shopping.

Assuming you are among the happy, well-heeled few who just happen to have a few thousand pounds, or dollars, burning a hole in your pocket, there is actually only one hotel hereabouts, the **Cala di Volpe** in **Porto Cervo**. For that is what a night's lodging costs in the presidential suite of this palace, where such leaders as Juan Carlos of Spain and the late King Hussein of Jordan have spent a lot of time, and other stars of the international jet set drop in regularly. Even more modest accommodation in this hotel will cost several hundred pounds a night.

The **Costa Smeralda** is a 3,000-hectare (7,413-acre) formerly deserted stretch of coastline which was transformed in the space of just a few years to a holiday paradise for the moneyed people, and their hangers-on. This carefully concocted Eldorado is, by and large, the work of the multi-millionaire Karim Aga Khan, who was the first to discover the Emerald Coast (as it is called in English) and open it up to the rich with his villas, apartments and hotels. This done, developers were given the green light for building along the rest of the 50-km (31-mile) stretch of coast. One vacation town after another has raised its artificial head.

The nerve centre of this synthetic creation is **Porto Cervo**, where the beautiful people meet one another on the Piazzetta. Alongside a supermarket, Armani, Versace and Cartier are represented in the nearby shopping arcade.

The **beaches**, naturally, are one of the highlights here. However, setting out in a boat is advisable if you want to find truly beautiful and remotely situated inlets on this still dream-like coast. There is no public ferry line calling at the smaller

The Porto Cervo yacht harbour

swimming beaches which are scattered about the islands: most of these are privately owned. Even if you are fortunate enough to own your own yacht, you must plan on spending extremely high daily dock fees. As a result, lesser mortals generally settle for a spot at **Long Beach**, the wind-sheltered bay of **Petra Manna** or **Capriccioli Bay**. A beach you really should visit is the **Romazzino**, also known as Princess Beach. It is not only especially safe, but you can also have a fine lunch here in the beach restaurant of the **Romazzino Hotel** (tel: 0789 977111). Perhaps the most famous and appealing beach of all is the **Spiaggia Rosa**: in the last three years it has not been accessible as it has become part of the National Sea Park protection programme.

The Costa Smeralda **Marina**, the best marina in Sardinia, was completed in 1975. Its wharf is among the best functioning in the world and there are 650 berths here for boats between 12 and 55 metres (38–176ft) in length as well as a special dry dock. The best-known regatta held here is the Settimana della Bocche, which takes place at the end of August. In uneven years, at the beginning of September, antique sailing boats converge at the port and a race is held in the straights of Bonifacio.

Naturally, the Costa Smeralda also has recreational facilities corresponding to the needs of its public. The 18-hole **Pevero Golf Club** (tel: 0789 96210) is considered one of the most beautiful in all Europe, but it is questionable whether one will be admitted. There are five tennis courts available and various sport facilities at the **Cervo Tennis Club** (tel: 0789 931612), and they are not the exclusive preserve of the rich and famous. If you book in adavance – and if tennis is your passion – it is also possible to stay at the club. It has 16 attractive rooms and, compared to most Costa Smeralda accommodation, is fairly reasonably priced.

The grand Cala di Volpe hotel

Even if some people claim there is nothing of historic interest to see here, you will find the *Mater Dolorosa* by El Greco in the **Chiesa di Stella Mares** in Porto Cervo, a gift from a German industrial family in gratitude for the recovery of their daughter from a serious illness. The 16th-century organ comes from Naples. In addition, the yachts – some of which have antiquarian value – are worth seeing. If your one-day outing turns into a longer visit, you may need some help deciding where to stay. There are five hotels of the Aga Khan's *Consorzio* to choose from. At the head of the list is, of course, the **Cala di Volpe**, with a mix of local and luxurious décor some people find stunning. The French architect Jacques Couelle has embodied in his design both a feel for nature and an air of exclusivity. As a guest, you will be ferried to the beach via the hotel's private boat. The **Cervo**, located directly in the centre of Porto Cervo, is a *bit* less expensive than the other lodgings listed here, and every room has a magnificent view of the sea. Its terrace bar is well known as a meeting place. The **Romazzino** overlooks the sea and has a magnificent, fragrant-flowering garden which slopes gently down to the beach. The **Pitrizza** consists of a cluster of villas whose terraces and gardens provide guests with peace and quiet and proximity to nature. Again, the prices are beyond the reach of most visitors. You can eat and drink well on the Costa Smeralda but apart from a few notable excpetions, it is no mecca for gourments. Specialities always include fish, *spaghetti aragosta*, roast suckling pig from the barbecue and smoked wild boar ham. If you need a change of scene, try an excursion to San Pantaleo, or **Porto Rotondo**, a small-scale Porto Cervo about 20 minutes away by car. The resort was built in 1963 and although it is less attractive architecturally it is still stylish. It lies in a little bay, with tiny *piazzas*, a few designer boutiques, a small harbour and two white sandy beaches. The architect Andrea Cascella designed the pretty church of San Lorenzo, up the steps leading off the central Piazzetta San Marco.

Accommodation

(Dialling Code 0789)

CALA DI VOLPE☆☆☆☆L
Loc. Cala di Volpe
Tel: 976111; fax: 976617
www.luxurycollection.com
PITRIZZA☆☆☆☆L
Loc. Liscia di Vacca
Tel: 930111; fax: 930611
www.luxurycollection.com
ROMAZZINO☆☆☆☆L
Tel: 977111; fax: 977618
GOLF HOTEL☆☆☆
Loc. Cala di Volpe
Tel: 96650; fax: 971087
www.bluhotel.it
CERVO☆☆☆
Tel: 931111; fax: 931613
CERVO TENNIS CLUB☆☆☆
Tel: 931612
CAPRIOCCIOLI☆☆☆
Loc. Capriccioli
Tel: 96004; fax: 96422
NIBARU☆☆☆
Loc. Cala di Volpe
Tel: 96038; fax: 96474
www.hotelnibaru.it
PICCOLO PEVERO☆☆☆
Golfo Pevero
Tel: 94551; fax: 92683
www.piccolopevero.it
PICCOLO GOLF☆☆☆
Cala di Volpe
Tel: 965520; fax: 96565
www.ilpiccologolf.com
VALDIOLA☆☆☆
Loc. Porto Cervo
Tel: 96215; fax: 96652
www.wel.it
VILLA SOPRAVENTO☆☆
Loc. Porto Cervo
Tel: 94717; fax: 907380

Baia Sardinia
GRAND HOTEL SMERALDO BEACH☆☆☆
Tel: 99046; fax: 99500
www.iti.hotels.it

LA ROCCA
Tel: 933131; fax: 933059
DELLE VIGNE
Via Mucchi Bianchi
Tel: 950066; fax: 950069
www.renabianca.com

Restaurants

There is no shortage of good places to eat:
GALLURA
Corso Umberto 145
Olbia
Tel: 24648
GAMBERO
Via Lamarmora 6
Olbia
Tel: 23874
IL BARETTO
Piazzetta Rudalza
Tel: 34017
IL PESCATORE
Molo Vecchio
Porto Cervo
Tel: 92296
ROSEMARY
Loc. Liscia di Vacca
Porto Cervo
Tel: 91185

Gennargentu

TOUR 16

In the Heart of Gennargentu

A day in Nuoro and its environs; sightseeing in the city of Orgosolo; overnight stay in the Hotel Su Gologone.

Nuoro is a peculiar city which keeps a grip on its characteristically reserved and gruff reputation. It is even a challenge to get there in the first place. When you drive up the superhighway from Oristano, past the Lago Omodeo and the industrial complex of Ottana, there *are* direction signs for Nuoro. But you can seek the city in vain if not forewarned. It is expertly hidden behind a hill. If you miss the exit ramp and traverse the tunnel, you will have to add an extra 20km (12 miles) to your trip. If you come from the opposite direction – from Siniscola and Posada – Nuoro appears high above you on the mountain, a defiant fortress revealing precious little of itself. The city is most forbidding, though, when approached via the road from Orgosolo and Oliena. Multi-storey housing projects block the narrow space between the cliffs like a dam, accentuating the remote mood of the place. What's more, if you are leaving warm and humid Oristano or the beaches of San Teodoro, driving into the drizzling rain which is so common up here, you will probably want to turn around right away.

No one comes to Nuoro for its cultural and historical charm, nor for its picturesque appearance. Its ambience echoes that of Barbagia, Sardinia's mountain region, and the people here seem reserved and suspicious. However, two aspects of the city make it worth visiting. The internationally renowned Nobel Prize-winning author **Grazia Deledda** grew up in Nuoro, and there is an interesting folklore museum located here, the Museo della Vita e delle Tradizione Sarde, housing a rich and comprehensive collection of folk artefacts.

Grazia Deledda wrote her first stories when she was very young – the first at the age of 15 – taking as subject matter the life and customs of the people of Nuoro and the surrounding villages. The stories were written from the point of view of a somewhat injured insider, getting her own back on her contemporaries. For the character of Angelo de Gubernatis' journal, *Rivista delle Tradizioni Popolari Italiane* (*Review of Italian Folk Traditions*), she gathered – and when necessary translated – the aphorisms of the people of Nuoro and its environs: curses and maledictions, adages and maxims, as well as *attitos* (funeral hymns). She collected material

In Gennargentu near Oliena

about local beliefs and superstitions, folk medicine, greetings and formulaic congratulations, funeral customs, charitable traditions, festivals and poetry. This project proved the cornerstone for her comprehensive investigation of the folkloric traditions of the region, and a source of inspiration for original works she would write many years later in Rome. Her subsequent publications, such as *Fior di Sardinia,* as well as articles published in Italian and Sardinian magazines, earned her the enmity of some, but they also secured her a place in the intellectual pantheon of Sardinia and Italy. Later, when Deledda married and was living with her family in Rome, the books drawing on her life on Sardinia kept appearing. The themes of her work always revolve around life and death, the rugged landscape of the Barbagia, and the taciturn stoicism of its people. Deledda was the first author to distil and disseminate a picture of Sardinia and its people, and she has been largely responsible for moulding our impressions of the culture.

The house where she was born is located at Via Deledda 42, where the building has been remodelled and made into a small museum, the **Casa di Grazia Deledda** (open in summer; 9am–1pm; 3–7pm in winter; admission charge).

Your second destination is the **Museo della Vita e delle Tradizione Sarde**, Via Mereu 56 (open in summer; 9am–1pm, 3–7pm in winter; admission charge). Its 18 rooms provide a comprehensive view of Sardinian tradition and culture, crafts and customs. There are, for example, three rooms filled with masks from the *Carneval* (Mardi Gras) celebrations in the Barbagia. The museum complex is designed to evoke a Sardinian village. Further sights in town include the **Cattedrale di Nostra Signora della Neve** (Our Lady of the Snows) which houses a large collection of valuable art treasures.

After so much cultural inspiration you may need a bit of restoration. If so, drive up the **Monte Ortobene** – the annual goal of the *Sagra del Rendentore* (Festival of the Redeemer) in August; in a slow procession, the congregation approaches the huge statue of Christ on the summit. The Belvedere, the observation platform on the Monte Ortobene, gives some of the best views on the island. The view extends from the rugged cliffs of the Sopramonte at Dorgali out to the high plain of Bitti with its extensive forests of cork-oak.

The best place to eat in Nuoro is the **Canne al Vento**, named after the best-known novel by Grazia Deledda. It is renowned for its traditional cuisine: try roast suckling pig, and some of their delicious *pecorino* cheese. Thus fortified, you can look forward to your afternoon activities.

Orgosolo still lives on the ominous reputation for banditry earned in decades past, when it was the home of a number of notorious bandits. Just a couple of decades ago it was customary to carry firearms here – usually shotguns. And a film called *The Bandits of Orgosolo* by Vittorio de Seta helped keep the lawless reputation alive. However, this romanticisation of banditry makes it is easy to gloss over the historical and social conditions which compelled local shepherds and farmers to formulate their own code. Stroll through the village, which has expanded in recent years, and sometimes you feel you are in a socially aware open-air art gallery. Orgosolo is famous for its provocative murals, painted on walls and stairs by Sardinian artists since the middle of the 1970s. At that time the central theme given expression in these murals was resistance to Italian patronage. The political theses of groups like the Baader-Meinhof gang or the Red Brigade also influenced some of this work. During the years that these paint-

Social and political commentary, al fresco

Authentic Gennargentu 'salon': the village square

ings have decorated the walls of the village, anxieties about the difficult living conditions of the shepherds crop up again and again. Land theft, the power of large estate owners, unjust economic policies and insufficient consideration for the shepherds' traditional way of life – all these issues appear in the murals. Today the revolutionary fervour is more muted, and while some of the political graffiti of Orgosolo is a heartfelt protest against injustice, some of it is art for art's sake.

The road at the foot of the Sopramonte winds through an idyllic landscape to **Oliena**. Located by the **Fontana Su Gologone**, the largest spring in the country, is an exclusive hotel of the same name. Despite its stylish atmosphere and high prices, you won't get the feeling you have landed in some sterile luxury bunker. The rooms are tastefully furnished with traditionally crafted trunks, beds and carpets. There is a freshwater swimming pool – a real symbol of luxury on water-poor Sardinia – tennis courts, riding excursions and guided hikes through the wonderful surroundings of Barbagia. A visit to the **caves** located in the area, the **Su Bentu** cave perhaps, or the Nuragic village of **Tiscali** in the **Lanaittu Valley**, are some obvious side trips to make while you are here. Tiscali is a Nuragic village discovered in a collapsed grotto and has become a very popular walk. Ask at the hotel reception desk for more detailed information about the path which leads there.

This is a good place for an overnight stop, especially as the hotel restaurant serves excellent traditional Sardinian and Italian cuisine. But you should also make one more excursion from here (perhaps the following morning as your day has been a full one), to nearby **Dorgali**, to taste the local Cannonau red wine, which is at its best here. Just outside Dorgali is the spectacular **Gola di Gorropu**, the only canyon in Europe, its sheer vertical slopes dropping over 300m (984ft) to the ground below.

Accommodation

If you want to stay at the Su Gologone, the best available accommodation in this region, make prior reservations, especially during summer and on major holidays. If you find it is fully booked, here are some recommended alternatives:

(Dialling Code 0784)

EURO HOTEL✩✩✩
Viale Trieste,
Nuoro
Tel: 34071
Fax: 33643

PARADISO✩✩✩
Via Aosta,
Nuoro
Tel: 35585
Fax: 232782

SANDALIA✩✩✩
Via Einaudi,
Nuoro
Tel/fax: 38353

GRILLO✩✩✩
Via Mons.Melas 14,
Nuoro
Tel: 38678
Fax: 32005

SU GOLOGONE✩✩✩✩
Loc. Su Gologone,
Oliena
Tel: 287512
Fax: 287668

MONTE MACCIONE✩✩✩
Oliena
Tel: 288363
Fax: 288473

QUERCETO
Via Lamarmora
Dorgali

Tel: 96509
Fax: 95254

Restaurants

The Canne al Vento and the Su Gologone, already described in the itinerary text, are the best places to eat out, but the other establishments listed below are also recommended:

CANNE AL VENTO
Viale Repubblica 65
Nuoro
Tel: 201762

DA GESUINO
Viale Ciusa
Nuoro
Tel: 34140

DA GIOVANNI
Via IV Novembre 9
Nuoro
Tel: 30562

SU GOLOGONE
Loc. Su Gologone
Tel: 287512

TESTONE
Agriturismo
Tel: 73954
Open only with reservation.

C&K
Via Martin Luther King 2/4
Oliena
Tel: 288024

Beaches

Sardinia is justly famous for its beaches. Without doubt, the island has the most beautiful coastline in all of Italy, if not the entire Mediterranean basin. The algae which plagues so many Mediterranean beaches has not yet arrived here, and there are the added enticements of white sand, rose-coloured cliffs and water of the deepest blue. Many beautiful beaches and inlets are still freely accessible, and relatively few coastal regions have been opened up to mass tourism. Driving many kilometres in order to discover a secluded little beach of your own is therefore completely unnecessary. The following rule of thumb applies to all of Sardinia: the closer you are to one of the larger ferry harbours, the more crowded the beaches. (And the closer to the Costa Smeralda, the more expensive *everything* is.)

Chia and the Costa del Sud: located just under an hour's drive west of Cagliari are the huge sand dunes of Chia, which you can reach via the SS195. Only surfers make use of the strong winds at the Capo Spartivento. Otherwise, this long, white beach is relatively untouched by the ravages of tourism. The rocky bays of the Costa del Sud between Capo Spartivento and Capo Teulada are equally as pristine and deserted. Although some people steadfastly remain infatuated with the Costa Smeralda, it is just as beautiful here, if not more so. Little side roads – where you can park your car –

Capo Cáccia

The red cliffs of Arbatax

lead off from the Strada Panoramica to the sea. From there, you can seek out your very own private bay, sometimes even with a bit of sandy beach. The panorama is rounded out harmoniously by coastal watchtowers and the little islands which lie along the coast. You will search in vain, though, for bars and discos here.

Isola di Sant Antioco: the Spiaggia Grossa of Calasetta on the Isola di Sant Antioco, near the *tonnara*, has a beautiful white sand beach in a large rounded bay with a view of the Isola di San Pietro which lies across from it. The *camera della morte*, a little inlet adjacent to the *tonnara,* is the end of the line for tuna during the season. The rest of the year, it is a paradise for holidaymakers and the sun-hungry, nestled amid luxuriant vegetation.

Fontanamare and Cala Domestica: Fontanamare the former port for shipping Sulcis coal from the mines of Iglisiente, stands abandoned today and has a lovely white sand beach. You get to it by taking the SS130 and turning off shortly after Gonessa. The asphalted road, which leads to a huge car park by the sea, runs parallel to a dried-up river valley, overgrown with reed-grass. Just past this begins one of the most gorgeous coastal roads, with a view over the Pan di Zucchero to Nebida and Masau.

The stretch to the Cala Domastica at Buggeru is a bit more complicated. Starting out from Cagliari, you first face the long drive up through Iglesias (SS130) and Fluminimaggiori (SS126). At the Ponte Riu Sessini, the road goes down to Buggeru. There you will find every variation of shoreline formation, from steep craggy cliffs to flat beaches. The monastic seclusion between the Capo Pecora and the Cala Domestica is ideal for people who don't enjoy the bustle of tourist centres.

Piscinas and Costa Verde: both these beaches are reached by way of the SS126. At the village of Guspini, the road turns off in a westerly direction. The coast between Piscinas and Marina di Arbus has dream-like beaches which are still not overrun. The road that parallels the coast certainly makes access easy. Further to the north among the huge sand dunes you may have to share

The coast near San Teodoro

your beach with bathers from the holiday villages, such as Torre dei Corsari. However, even if others do turn up here in somewhat increasing numbers, they are still quite unobtrusive when compared to the masses congregated on the northeast coast.

Capo Mannu – Is Arenas: huge sand dunes several kilometres long extend north of Oristano, reached via the SS292. If you undertake a long hike you will find some truly isolated spots here.

Porto Conte: this virtually circular swimming bay to the north of Alghero is certainly no secret, but its flat beach and shady pine forest make it ideal for families with children.

The Beach of Stintino: located on the most extreme northwestern tip of the island, this beach seduces you with its shimmering turquoise water. Unfortunately, the scene is marred a bit by the nearby industrial area of Porto Torres. Also, the building craze has made rather heavy inroads here and transformed a former *tonnara* into a holiday village.

Isola Rossa and Costa Paradiso: for those who have the good fortune to rent a cottage on the Costa Paradiso, their holiday is in the bag. Deep blue and turquoise waters and bizarrely formed rose-hued cliffs do complete justice to the name Costa Paradiso. Unfortunately, the most picturesque areas are the private beaches of large holiday settlements, so that the rest of us must make do with the stretch of coast across from the Isola Rossa on the Punte di Canneddi.

Porto Istana: here, to the south of Olbia, you are right in the middle of Sardinia big time: noise and people. If you have got off course somehow and ended up here, you can still find a beautiful sandy beach with a view across to the island of Tavolara. On a neighbouring beach in Porto San Paolo, the bay is punctuated by the skeletons of two shipwrecks. It is picturesque and not completely overrun – yet. This is, however, a real alternative to the completely packed beaches around San Teodoro.

Cala Gonone: this former counter-culture paradise on the east coast has, in recent times, become quite heavily commercialised. If you do not have your own boat, the only way to reach a remote bay is with the commuter boat convoy – but you will have to share your find. If you want to be completely undisturbed, you are better off undertaking a long hike and walking down to the rocky coast at Baunei. The beaches at Santa Maria di Navarrese and the red cliffs beside the ferry harbour of Arbatax are also attractive.

Costa Rei: this stretch of coast, located to the east, and its northern extension, such as the beaches at Muravera, have been discovered for a long time now. However, the Costa Rei still has quiet beaches and gleaming white sand – as long as you keep your distance from the settlements around Monte Nai. Bordering on this coastal area is farmland – there are no bars in sight.

Villasimius: solitude here has long been a thing of the past. Despite this, the village with its wonderful beaches has lost none of its attraction. And, in comparison to San Teodoro, it has preserved its charm as well. Just a few kilometres to the north, it is much quieter on the long sand beaches of the Capo Carbonara.

Special Events

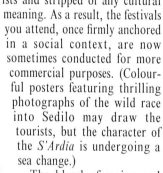

Hardly a day passes on Sardinia without a festival being celebrated somewhere on the island. Visitors who want to plan their itineraries around specific celebrations and holidays should go to the tourist offices and pick up a brochure which lists all these events and provides exact dates. There are probably more than 1,000 holidays and festivals observed annually on the island, so visitors should be able to join in the festivities no matter what time of year they come.

Sardinia does not have a single, monolithic culture, and quite different customs are practised in different regions. Each area has its own unique social structures, traditions and customs. Many of these subcultures, however, are on the verge of dying out or losing their authenticity, their age-old rites replaced by artificially concocted ceremonies staged for tourists and stripped of any cultural meaning. As a result, the festivals you attend, once firmly anchored in a social context, are now sometimes conducted for more commercial purposes. (Colourful posters featuring thrilling photographs of the wild race into Sedilo may draw the tourists, but the character of the *S'Ardia* is undergoing a sea change.)

The blend of major and minor chords in these festivals perseveres, however. You will still experience an uncommon mixture of mourning and merriment, especially in the *ballu tundo*, the circle dance introduced to the world by Grazia Deledda's novel, *Canne al Vento,* and later, by the film of the same name. Accompanied by archaic *launeddas* – reed pipes – the dancers move

Easter in Arbatax

The Sagra di Sant'Efisio in Cagliari

in a rhythmic triple step. In earlier times, they danced around a large bonfire. The rendering of the *ballu tundu* on a pillar in the medieval chapel of San Pietro di Zuri is evidence that the dance dates from before 1291. It is assumed, however, that its origins lie still further in the past. The *launeddas*, or shepherds' pipes, which are still used today, date from very ancient times. It is possible they were used as musical instruments by the Nuraghi people. This continuity, the firm grip maintained on what are sometimes truly ancient traditions, is typical of Sardinian culture in general.

Most of the festivals revolve around a *sagre*, a religious celebration held in honour of a saint, for the most part local patron saints. These village ceremonies often involve days of preparation and are carried out strictly according to the rules of tradition. Free meals offered to guests – as at San Francesco di Lula – are an exception rather than the rule at these festivals.

It is interesting to note the proximity of today's Christian shrines to the places revered by earlier religions, the water temples of the Nuragic, for example. Often, the Nuragic sites now bear Christian names, such as Santa Barbara, Santu Antine (Constantine) and so on. Through the centuries, Christian churches have been established on pagan cult sites. In San Salvatore on the Sinis Peninsula, for example, the original Nuragic water temple is found amid the subterranean arches of a church. There is another tradition alive and well on Sardinia, as well, one that preserves elements of the island's archaic, pre-Christian civilisation. Sometimes, in the midst of purportedly Catholic celebrations, such as the protracted annual parish festivals, when pilgrims are housed in little lodges called *muristenes*, visitors will feel they are taking part in events that have changed little over thousands of years.

During the *sagre,* one also has an opportunity to see and admire the colourful and costly traditional Sardinian costumes – beautifully embroidered skirts in Oliena, Catalan lace in Alghero, the simple costumes of the men of Cabras, and the elaborate lace brocade worn by the women of Quartucciu. It is hard to imagine any other

Running the S'ardia in Sedilo

Mediterranean island having such a diversity of festival costumes. Those who want a closer look can see a large number of these garments in the Museo della Vita e delle Tradizione Popolari in Nuoro, and get an overview of their variety and opulence.

The carnival festivities (better known to many as Mardi Gras) of Sardinia are certainly a high point on the island calendar of events. Of particular interest among these is the *Sartiglia* in **Oristano**, a competition held by contestants dressed in historical costume. The archaic ceremonies accompanying the masked parades in **Mamoiada** and **Ottana** are equally impressive. *Mamuthones* clothed in hides and draped in bells oppose hunters armed with lassoes. The river city of **Bosa** has a truly boisterous carnival parade which has become more and more popular in recent years.

Easter is another important event in the Sardinian year, celebrated with processions and parades in many towns. Frequently,

the processions of black-hooded men last through the night. Among these, the *Lunissanti* (Holy Monday) celebrations in **Castelsardo** and Good Friday festivities in **Alghero** are especially prominent. In an elaborate procession of lights – the origins of which date from the city's Spanish period – the Descent from the Cross is simulated. Accompanied by a brass band playing sacred music, the long procession, with the women in their traditional Spanish *mantillas*, moves through the old quarter of the town to the cathedral. Impressive processional marches also take place in **Sassari**, **Cagliari**, **Nuoro** and **Oliena**.

The *Sagra di Sant'Efisio,* held in May in **Cagliari**, is dedicated to that city's patron saint and is the most famous celebration on the island. The effigy of the saint is carried on a richly decorated ox cart to the tiny church of Pula, on the spot where he was martyred. The *Cavalcata Sarda* in **Sassari** is a holiday parade with riding competitions and various other entertainments, and people dressed in ethnic local costumes, which was re-established nearly 50 years ago by the Rotary Club.

There is plenty of excitement to be had at the *S'ardia* on 6 and 7 July in **Sedilo**, where a truly spectacular horse race takes place, finishing in front of the Chiesa di San Constantino. The *S'ardias* never come to an end without dangerous accidents – sometimes with fatal results.

August is a particularly rich month for festivals. The candle festival, *Candelieri,* in **Sassari** (14 August) and the procession *L'assunta* in **Orgosolo** (15 August) are impressive displays of traditional and colourful ethnic costumes. One month later, in September, is the **Sagre de San Salvatore**, during which a sacred statue is carried from Cabras to the church of San Salvatore on the **Sinis Peninsula**, by barefoot runners.

The only quiet seasons of the year are autumn and winter. But there are exceptions even then: **Christmas** and **New Year** festivities, although mainly family occasions, tend to spill out onto the street.

Dining

There is a persistent and odious rumour that the cuisine on Sardinia is not quite up to scratch. This is quite simply a patent falsehood since, in most cases, and most places during the high season, it is possible to find outstanding food here, although not always at reasonable prices. As is true throughout Italy, it is a good idea to acquaint yourself with the institution of *pane e coperto*, or 'bread and place setting'. For these two necessities, plan on an additional charge being added to your bill *over and above* the charges for table service. Thus, the prices on the menus do not correspond to those you actually pay. When ordering fish remember that the price displayed on the menu is per 100g (4oz) and therefore has to be multiplied accordingly. The other thing you should know about eating out on Sardinia is that there are several names, and categories, for dining establishments, which indicate the prices charged within.

A *ristorante* is an up-market restaurant which can sometimes be rather expensive. *Trattorias* are, for the most part, simple traditional bistros which frequently serve food of outstanding quality. Finally, *pizzerias* offer the most simple fare, and the usual three courses are not obligatory.

But what characterises the cuisine of Sardinia? One special feature is its ample use of meat which, in the Mediterranean basin, is very unusual. That is not to say that you should choose meat dishes over those using fish. Any island that boasts a 'lobster coast' has diverse seafood specialities on offer. However, one should not forget that Sardinia consists, to a large extent, of pasture lands where herds of livestock graze, a fact that is borne out in the indigenous cuisine.

Sardinia also has a reputation for bread, in all its rich variety. You will find everything here from the former 'poor people's bread', which is made of acorns, to the *pane integrale* (wholemeal bread). The best known however, is the *pane carasau* or *carta da musica*, the thinnest sort of flat bread, which the shepherds still take with them on their long treks through the country. Nowadays, it is served in most restaurants, whether modest or expensive.

Better known than the Sardinian bread, though, is the island's cheese: it is not only the renowned *pecorino* that enjoys a worldwide reputation. You should try, for example, *caprino*, *fiore sardo*, *calcagno* and *bonassai*, to name only a few varieties. From the fresh cheese or curd to the sharp well-aged *pecorino,* the cheeses will afford you a voyage of culinary discovery. If you happen to see a cheese seller by the side of the road and are able to use a whole cheese weighing between 1 and 2 kgs (2.2–4.4lbs), you should go ahead and buy it.

Of the starters *(antipasti)* on the menu, *antipasti di terra* is the most typically Sardinian. These dishes consist primarily of chunks of salted meat and sausage (or, if you are very lucky, wild boar or venison), plus olives, chicken livers and tripe. If you are unable to resist bread soup or hearty bean soup, then you have come to the right place. Among the pasta dishes – so popular on the mainland – one should try here *malloreddus* – the Sardinian version of *gnocchi*, and the tasty *ravioli* – dumplings with ricotta cheese. *Culingionis* (dumplings of flour and potato batter), *maccarones cravaos* (larger dumplings) and *maccarones de busa* (a type of very fine canneloni) are also very popular. Most pasta dishes are served in a sauce of fresh tomatoes, with chunks of meat or sausage and delicate herbs and spices. Another dish that appears frequently on Sardinian menus is *spaghetti bottariga*, pasta with fish roe, equal here in price and prestige to caviar.

Main courses on Sardinia characteristically consist of *arrosti*, or roasted meat. The type of meat varies, according to the season, alternating between lamb, veal, pork and wild boar. Celery, fennel and potatoes are served as side dishes. *Piselle e carciofi*, boiled artichokes with peas, is an unusual and delicious combination.

If you are staying overnight in Alghero, you should try 'Catalan lobster'. Fresh tuna, and *pesce spada* (swordfish) are also hard to resist. And many beach and harbour-side restaurants serve plates of plain grilled fish, fresh from the sea that morning, which are hard to beat.

For dessert you should order a *dolci sardi*, which simply means a Sardinian sweet, which is interpreted differently depending on the region. You should sample these little delicacies in several towns at bakeries and *pasticerias*. A popular dessert, for those who have no interest whatsoever in losing weight, is a *sebada*: two rounds of pastry are dipped in honey, filled with curd cheese, sprinkled with sugar and deep fried. If this all sounds too much, you could choose from a selection of seasonal fruit which is usually offered at the end of a meal, or try a mixture of dried fruit and nuts.

If you are partial to *digestifs,* you might take well to one of the especially strong Sardinian versions of *aquavit*. The secret is to reach for a bottle with no label. Take note, however, that D.H. Lawrence, who visited the island in 1921 and wrote about it so eloquently in *Sea and Sardinia*, described *aquavit* as resembling 'sweetened petroleum with a dash of aniseed: filthy'.

Just as beneficial to digestion, and much better tasting, is *liquore di mirto*, a herbal liqueur distilled from myrtle which

is popular throughout the island. It is available in several varieties, ranging from a reddish-colour if the myrtle berries have been used, to a clear liquid if only the leaves have gone into the brew.

Any of the local wines are a good choice, particularly if you like heavy and earthy flavours. The best, and best-known, are the *Cannonau* wines, made in the provinces of Cagliari, Sassari and Nuoro. The light *Vermentino* wines from around Cagliari are also recommened, as is the fine, dry *Spumanti*, and the *Malvasia*, a sweet desert wine. The beer here is still 'developing'. The local Ichnusa beer tastes a bit unusual, but is quite good.

If you really want to avoid any element of culinary chance, take the recommendations given at the end of the various tours, or stick with the restaurants listed below, which are among the best in Sardinia. At these places you are sure to find both Italian and traditional Sardinian cuisine, both of consistently high quality. On the other hand, making discoveries of your own is part of the holiday experience, and in most parts of Sardinia the experience is likely to be a good one.

CANNE AL VENTO
Viale Repubblica 66
Nuoro
Tel: (0784) 201762
(Closed Sunday)
Try the roast suckling pig and finish your meal with *pecorino* cheese.

GIAMARANTO
Via Alghero 69
Sassari
Tel: (079) 274598
(Closed Sunday in August)
Sassari's best: try the ravioli with artichokes followed by the lobster salad. A fine list of Sardinian wines complements anything you may choose from the menu.

DA NICOLO
Corso Cavour 32
Caroloforte
Tel: (0781) 854048
Family-run, in the centre of town. The fish-filled ravioli and tuna in a Ligurian (Genoese) sauce are specialities.

IL FARO

Via Bellini 25
Oristano
Tel: (0783) 70002
Elegant restaurant serving seafood specialties and lamb with mint sauce prepared by one of the island's top chefs. Good deserts and excellent local wines.

LILLICU
Via Sardegna 78
Tel: (070) 652970
Reservation necessary. Renowed for seafood and grilled fish, but will also serve meat.

SA FUNTA
Via Garibaldi 25

Cabras
Tel: (0783) 290685
Water comes from the well in the middle of the restaurant. Good loacl dishes include smoked mullet, *freula* (local couscous in fish broth), spaghetti with limpet sauce, and sole in walnut sauce. Try the unusual herbal drinks.

DAL CORSARO
Viale Regina Margherita 28
Cagliari
Tel: (070) 370295
One of the finest restaurants in the island serving excellent fish and meat dishes. Good wine list.

LO SCOGLO
Capo S. Elia, Loc. Calamosca
Cagliari
Tel: (070) 3911727
(Closed Sunday)
A highly renowned restaurant. Its speciality is delicious oven-baked fish.

SU GOLOGONE
Loc. Su Gologone
Oliena, Nuoro
Tel: (0784) 287512
(Closed in February)
Elegant restaurant in the hotel of the same name; serves traditional Sardinian dishes as well as very good mainland-Italian food.

GALLURA
Corso Umberto 145
Olbia
Tel: (0789) 24648
Renowned throughout the island for excellent quality. Try *burrida ai pinoli* (catfish with pine kernels), sea truffle and date soup, lobster salad and *mormora al cartoccio* (fish cooked in a bag). Good wine list. Closed Monday.

SA CARDIGA E SU SCHIRIONI
Capoterra – SS195
10km (6 miles) from Cagliari
Tel: (070) 71652/2
(Closed Monday)
Vies with Dal Corsaro for the title of the finest seafood restaurant on the island.

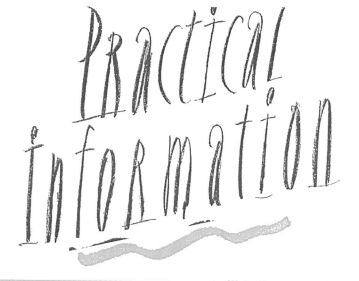

PRACTICAL information

When to Go

When should you go to Sardinia? Actually, any time is a good time, since every season has its own attractions. In general, summer on the island is very hot. Winter, in the southern half of Sardinia, is usually pleasantly warm although in the north there are frequent and heavy rains. In spring, with a bit of luck, you may be able to swim, though rather strong winds can also blow at this time of year. Autumn is generally delightful.

Unless you want to spend all your time on the beach, there are many advantages to going off-season. The island is far less crowded and hotels are not over-booked. In winter there are almost no tourists in Sardinia, and in January virtually the entire island is in bloom with a great profusion of colour. The disadvantage is that you may find many hotels, restaurants and museums closed.

Average Temperatures

(mean daily min/max)

	May	July	Sept	Dec
Alghero				
	11–23°C	19–29°C	17–26°C	8–16°C
	52–73°F	66–84°F	63–79°F	46–61°F
Cagliari				
	14–23°C	21–30°C	19–27°C	9–16°C
	57–73°F	70–86°F	66–81°F	48–62°F
Mountain Areas				
	2–12°C	15–22°C	15–25°C	0–6°C
	36–54°F	59–72°F	59–77°F	32–43°F

Water Temperatures

April	June	Aug	Sept	Oct
14°C	20°C	23°C	24°C	20°C
57°F	68°F	73°F	75°F	68°F

The *maestrale* is a strong wind which blows from the northeast. Its effects are most strongly felt in the northern part of the island, where its strength can be gauged by how far the cork-oaks lean away from the wind. To balance things out, the south experiences the hot and dry *scirocco* and the warm moist *libeccio*.

Visas

For residents of the European Union, the USA and Canada, a valid passport or personal identification card is sufficient, unless you are hoping to stay for more than three months. The usual rabies precautions for pets apply.

Custom Duties

As a rule, visitors arriving on Sardinia from the Italian mainland – that is, not via direct flights from or via Corsica – will already have cleared customs. The usual EU limits apply for Sardinia as well: 300 cigarettes, 3 litres of high proof spirits, 5 litres of wine.

Money Matters

As in the rest of Italy, the Italian Lira was replaced by the euro in January 2002. Travellers' cheques may also be cashed in most banks. If any of your cheques get lost or stolen, don't forget to cancel them. Credit cards are now accepted in most places throughout the island, and there are ATM machines in most towns, with instructions in several languages, including English.

TRANSPORTATION

By Air

The most important airports on the island are located at Cagliari (Elmas), Alghero (Fertilia) and Olbia. There are also several small airports, some of these open only in high season. Direct flights leave from London, and connections can be made from most European and American cities to all of the larger Italian airports (i.e. Rome, Milan, Genoa, Naples, Pisa and Venice), from where many flights connect with the island. For information contact:
Alitalia: from outside Europe tel: (800) 223 5730, www.alitaliausa.com. From the UK tel: (08705) 448259, www. alitalia. co.uk.
Meridiana: from outside Europe tel: (8488) 65643, reservations tel: (199) 111333, www.meridiana.it. From the UK tel: (0789) 52682. Direct flight from London Gatwick to Olbia three times a week from Easter–Oct.
British Airways: from outside Europe tel: (800) 223 5730, www.britishairways.com. From the UK tel: (0845) 773 377.
Ryanair: from the UK tel: (08701) 569 569, www.ryanair.com. Daily flights from London Stansted to Alghero.

Sea Connections

Daily ferries provide connections with Genoa, Civitavecchia (near Rome), Naples, Palermo and Livorno on the Italian mainland: These service the most important harbours on the island: Cagliari, Arbatax, Porto Torres and Olbia. Depending on the port of departure, the journey lasts between 8 and 12 hours. In summer, ferries also connect Cagliari/Palermo, Cagliari/Tunis and Cagliari/Trapani.
Tirrenia is the major ferry line (tel: 199 123199, from UK 081 3172999, www. tirrenia.it). Other ferry lines include:
Sardinia Ferries, tel: (019) 215511, fax: (019) 2155300, www.sardiniaferries.it.
Moby Lines, tel: (0789) 27927, fax: (0789) 27933, www.mobylines.it.

TRANSPORTATION

By Bus

Getting around by public transport can be a fascinating way of seeing the island, but if you are planning only a short stay it probably will not serve your purposes, as it is a very time-consuming way of travelling. Nevertheless, there is a good bus network which covers the entire island, including even the smallest villages in the remote areas of the Gennargentu. There is also an express bus network – called the *torpedoni* – which connects the most important cities. The following routes are served: Nuoro–Cagliari (3½ hrs); Sassari–Cagliari (4 hrs); and Nuoro–Sassari (2½ hrs). These times allow for intermediate stops; there is also a non-stop route between Cagliari and Sassari (3 hrs). The most reliable bus company is ARST, tel: (800) 865042, from the UK tel: (070) 4998324. Bus passes are available for two, three or four weeks.

In cities, buses are a good cheap method of transport. Buy tickets at the *giornali* stands which display a yellow 'Unione Sarda' banner. Make sure you stamp your ticket once you are on the bus.

By Train

The state-run railroad, Ferrovie dello Stato (FS), and Sardinian railways, Ferrovie della Sardegna, maintain the following railway routes: Cagliari–Sassari (4 hrs), Cagliari–Olbia (4 hrs), Cagliari–Oristano (1 hr), Oristano–Macomer (2½ hrs) and Cagliari–Iglesias (1 hr). The train ride from Cagliari into the Gennargentu Mountains is time-consuming but romantic. The route from Cagliari to Aritzo is especially recommended for train enthusiasts. The networks also schedule local trains between Nuoro–Macomer, Sassari–Alghero and Sassari–Palau and smaller places. Trenino Verde, tel: (800) 460220, from the UK tel: (070) 343112, www. treninoverde.com.

For further information on travelling by train, check at city stations, ask a travel agent or contact Ferrovie dello Stato (FS), tel: (8488) 892021 (only in Italy), www.fs.on-line.com.

Travelling by Car

Petrol is expensive in Sardinia. Make sure you fill your tank before heading off on long journeys – petrol stations are sparse away from towns and often close for lunch. The island has an unenviable record for road accidents, so you can either adopt a cautious approach or drive in the local style and hope for the best. Remember to take out the usual Green Card insurance before you leave home. European Union drivers just need their national licence; non-EU visitors need an International Licence.

Main Roads

The main road connecting the south of Sardinia with the north is the SS131 (Carlo Felice), with four lanes. It starts in Cagliari and reaches Porto Torres, passing by Oristano; near Abbasanta the road divides and a new branch now reaches Olbia: the SS131 bis. The other main road is the SS125 from Cagliari to Arzachena, following the coast; it is a slow road which can take longer than anticipated.

Parking

In large towns parking places are indicated by "blue stripes": each space is marked with a blue line indicating that you must pay. Look for an official with a blue badge and pay for the amount of time you need. Car theft is on the increase so take precautions.

Car Hire

Car hire is expensive in Sardinia. There are several local and international car rental firms at the airports, and many will also have offices in the larger Sardinian towns. It is a good idea to reserve a car in advance, particularly during the peak summer season. Rates can also be cheaper if booked with your flight and accommodation in a package.

Cagliari
Eurorent, Elmas Airport, tel: (070) 240129.
Avis, Elmas Airport, tel: (070) 240081.
Budget Rent-a-Car, Elmas Airport, tel: (070) 240310, fax: 070 240310.
Hertz Rent a Car, Elmas Airport, tel: (070) 240037.
Maggiore Rent-a-Car, Elmas Airport, tel: (070) 240069.

Alghero
Avis, Fertilia Airport, tel: (079) 935064.
Budget Rent-a-Car, Fertilia Airport, tel: (079) 935060.
Maggiore Rent-a-Car, Fertilia Airport, tel: (079) 935045.

Olbia
Avis, Costa Smeralda Airport, tel: (0789) 69540.
Budget Rent-a-Car, Costa Smeralda Airport, tel: (0789) 69605; fax: (0789) 66003.
Maggiore Rent-a-Car, Costa Smeralda Airport, tel: (0789) 69457.

HEALTH & EMERGENCIES

UK citizens with an E111 form (available from UK post offices: since 2005 each member of the family must have his or her own form) are entitled to reciprocal health facilities, but to cover all eventualities private insurance is recommended, as for all other nationalities. No special vaccinations are required before travelling to Sardinia. During summer you should take the usual precautions against sunburn and dehydration – use sunblock, wear a hat, cover up during the hottest periods, and drink plenty of water. Pharmacies are open, with a few exceptions in some localities, from 8.30am–noon and 4.30–7.30pm. Telephone 192 in Cagliari for information about pharmacies open out of hours.

Throughout Sardinia
Police 112
Ambulance 118
Automobile Club Italie 803 166

Public Holidays

January: New Year's Day (1st), Epiphany (6th)
March/April: Easter Sunday and Monday
April: Liberation Day (25th)
May: Labour Day (1st)
August: Assumption Day (15th)
November: All Saints' Day (1st)
December: Immaculate Conception (8th), Christmas Day (25th), Santo Stefano (26th)

Festivals

S. Antonio Abate: 16–17 January. Celebrated with large bonfires in almost every community. In Bortigali, Birori and Dualchi in Nuoro Province, it is celebrated on the Saturday and Sunday following the 17th.

S. Sebastiano: 19–20 January. Also celebrated in many communities.

Carnival/Mardi Gras: The *Sartiglia* in Oristano lasts from Sunday to Shrove Tuesday (Carnival/Mardi Gras). On these days as well, the famous masked parades are held in Mamoida and Ottana. The festivities in Bosa and Tempio Pausiania are held between Thursday and Shrove Tuesday.

Easter: In the following communities the Easter celebrations are of particular interest: Tergu, Castelsardo, Sassari, Alghero, Ittireddu and Oliena.

Sant' Efisio: 1 May. In Cagliari and Pula the festival honouring Cagliari's patron saint is celebrated.

Madonna dei Martiri: On the first Monday in June a festive procession on horseback takes place in Fonni.

S. Constantino: 7 July – a festival celebrated primarily at Sedilo with a wild horse race.

S. Maria della Neve: 5 August. Celebrated in Desulo. Festivities honouring S. Salvatore take place the following day in Nuoro. On the first Sunday of August the ship procession of St Maria del Mare

is celebrated in Bosa.

I Candelieri: 14 August – the high point of the festival year in Sassari.

L'Assunta: 15 August – especially interesting in the villages of Orgosolo, Ottana, Mamoiada and Dortgali.

Festival of the Redeemer: early September in San Salvatore, Sinis Peninsula.

The Festival of St Maria de Sauccu: 7–17 September – celebrated in Barbaggia in Bortigali. It includes traditional music and salvos of salutory gunshots.

Festival of S. Francesco: 4 October – in Ala di Sardi, a culinary extravaganza where everyone who comes as a pilgrim will be fed.

St Stephen's Day: 26 December.

USEFUL INFORMATION

Local Time

One hour ahead of Greenwich Mean Time (GMT). From late March to late October, time is advanced by 1hr (thus GMT +2).

Business Hours

Banks are open Monday–Friday 8.30am–1.30pm. Some main branches open again in the afternoon from 3–4.30pm, but don't count on it. As a rule, shops are open from 9am–1pm and 4.30–8pm. Only the Citta Mercati – the city shopping malls – stay open all day. Very few shops are open on Sunday.

Post & Telephone

Main branches of post offices are open Monday–Friday 8.30am–7.30pm, Saturday 8.30am–12.30pm. Stamps *(francobolli)* are also available at *tabacchi* shops displaying a black and white sign *valori e bollati*. They usually have a post box outside. Post boxes have two slots: one for city mail, one for all the rest.

There are bright orange telephone boxes all over the island and they are operated by phone cards – *carte telephonica*. You buy these cards at a *giornali* (newspaper stand). To phone abroad, first dial the international access code 00, then the country code: Australia (61), UK (44); US and Canada (1).

Electricity

Power sockets are rated at 220 volts and usually take 2-point plugs. An adaptor – usually available at airports – is useful.

Tipping

The tip – *la mancia* – is a matter of choice in Sardinian restaurants. Often a 10–15 percent service charge is added to your bill (as well as a cover charge). Extra tips for especially good service are of course appreciated, but not expected.

Taxi fares are fixed and metered – and tend to work out quite expensive – but no tip is expected.

Media

Newspapers: During the summer months you can find English and other foreign newspapers in most tourist centres, and in Cagliari and Sassari you will probably find some all year round, even if a day late. Even if you don't understand much Italian you may find the main Sardinian paper useful, because it has listings sections of what's on and where. It's called the *L'Unione Sarda* and can be found on any *giornali* stand.

Television: As well as the three national radio and television broadcasting channels run by RAI (Italian Radio and Television), there are numerous others. There are news bulletins almost every hour of the day, although the most popular are between 1 and 2pm and from 7 to 8.30pm. Cable television and Euro channels are also available, as well as satellite TV. TMC broadcasts the English channel Euro News in the morning (7am) and CNN from 2–7am.

Radio: There are numerous private radio stations, as well as the three national public stations (RAI UNO, DUE, TRE). Most are broadcast on stereo FM. In the northeast of the island, there are also English-language stations serving the

NATO bases. There are hourly traffic and weather bulletins on the RAI channels, in co-operation with ACI (Italian Automobile Association). In the summer these bulletins are broadcast in English, German and French.

TOURIST INFORMATION

Before you leave home:
The **Italian State Tourist Office** has offices in most major cities:
UK: 1 Princes Street, London W1R 8AY, tel: (020) 7408 1254; fax: (020) 7493 6695; website: www.enit.it, www.italian tourism.com
USA: 630 Fifth Avenue, Suite 1565, New York, NY 10111, tel: (212) 245 4822; fax: (212) 586 9249
Canada: 175 Bloor Street East, Suite 907, South Tower, Toronto M4W 3R8 tel: (416) 925 4882; fax: (416) 925 4799.

When you get to Sardinia:
Alghero
Piazza Portaterra 9
Tel: (079) 979054; fax: 974881
email: inoturism@infoalghero.it
Cagliari
ESIT (ENTE SARDO INDUSTRIE TURISMO)
Via Mameli 97
Tel: (070) 60231; fax: 664636
email: esiturismo@tiscali.it
www.esit.net
EPT (ENTI PROVINCIALE TURISMO)
Piazza Deffenu 9
Tel: (070) 604241; fax: 663207; free toll no. 800 203541
email: enturismoca@tiscali.it
www.tiscalinet.it/aast_ca
La Maddalena
Loc. Cala Gavetta
Tel: (0789) 736321; fax: 36655
Muravera
Via Macchiavelli 3
Tel: (070) 9930760; fax: 9931286; free toll: 800 258142
Nuoro
Piazza Italia 19
Tel: (0784) 30083; fax: 33432
email: info@enteturismo.nuoro.it
Olbia
Via Catello Piro 1.
Tel: (0789) 21453; fax: 22221
Oristano

Via Cagliari 278
Tel: (0783) 74191; fax: 302518
email: enturismo.orostano@tiscalinet.it
Palau
Via Nazionale 94
Tel: (0789) 709570; fax: 709570
email: imdpalau@tiscali.it
Sassari
EPT (ENTI PROVINCIALE TURISMO)
Viale Caprera 36
Tel: (079) 299544; fax: 299415
Fertilia Alghero Airport: tel/fax: 935124
AZIENDE AUTONOMA SOGGIORNO E
TOURISMO
Viale Umberto 72
Tel: (079) 233534; fax: 237585
email: aastss@tiscalinet.it
www.regione.sardegna.it/azstss

SPORT

Golf

Sardinia has four excellent 18-hole golf courses:
PEVERO GOLF CLUB, Cala di Volpe, Costa Smeralda, tel: (0789) 96210.
IS MOLA GOLF CLUB, S. Margherita di Pula, Cagliari, tel: (070) 9241013.
Is Arenas Golf and Country Club, Narbolia, tel: (0783) 52254.
Puntaldia, Punta Sabbatino, San Teodoro, tel: (0784) 864477.

Horse Riding

You can take half-day outings, whole-day trips, or tours lasting several days. Many hotels offer riding excursions. Information is available at local tourist agencies, at ESIT in Cagliari, or from ANTE **Sardegna** (Riders' Association), Via Pasteur 4, Cagliari tel: (070) 305816.

Trekking

Trekking is a great way to discover the hidden areas of the Nuorese and Iglesiente regions. The Supramonte in the Barbagia region is one of the best hiking areas in the island and hiking tours into the mountains of Aritzo are also possible. For most such excursions it is a good idea to hire the services of a guide who should be a member of the GAE (Guide Ambientali Escursionistiche). Contact the EPT tourist agency for details.

Diving

There are around 80 diving centres around the island, the highest concentration being on the northeast coast. Activities range from night diving to underwater photography. The marine parks make Sardinia a great natural aquarium. The parks are: Capo Carbonara-Villasimius (Cagliari Province); Golfo di Orosei (Nuoro Province); Tavolara-Capo Coda Cavallo (Sassari Province); Arcipelago della Maddalena (National Park, Sassari Province); Isola Asinara (National Park, Sassari Province); Capo Caccia-Porto Conte (Sassari Province); Sinis-Mal di Ventre (Oristano Province). For details of dive centres contact the EPT tourist agency.

Other Watersports

If you want to rent a boat, contact one of the following outfits:
OCCHIONI, in all main piers from Baia Sardinia to Porto Cervo, tel: (0336) 867049 or 3683 605692.
CRUISING CHARTER, Porto Rotondo, Cagliari, tel: (0789) 25944; fax: 25966; www.cruisingcharter.it.
The tourist agency has a free map showing Sardinia's ports.

If you want to learn how to sail, Caprera has one of the most reputable schools in Europe:
CENTRO VELICO CAPRERA, Loc. Punta Coda, Caprera, tel: (0789) 738529 or you could try the **Yacht Club**, Marina Piccola, Cagliari, tel: (070) 373099.

Windsurfing has become hugely popular, as the weather is ideal. You can rent a windsurf board practically anywhere on the island. The beaches of Santa Teresa di Gallura, the most northerly community, is a great place for both windsurfing and diving. Down in the south, surfers head for the strong winds of the Capo Spartivento, near Chia. Poetto is the mecca for windsurfers.

Index

H, I, J, K

L

M

ART/PHOTO CREDITS

Design Concept	V Barl
Cover Design	Klaus Geisler
Cartography	Berndtson & Berndtson
Photography by	Joachim Chwaszcza *and*
76	Dirk Hoffmann
17, 55, 79	Oliviero Olivieri
82, 95T	Rainer Pauli
21, 23B, 40, 42T, 61, 63, 79, 86, 87, 105	Jörg Reuther
2–3, 30, 39, 41B, 83, 95B, 101	Franco Stefan Ruiu
Cover	Robert Harding Picture Library
Back Cover	B Gradnik

L APA PUBLICATIONS

Part of the Langenscheidt Publishing Group

DISCOVERY CHANNEL

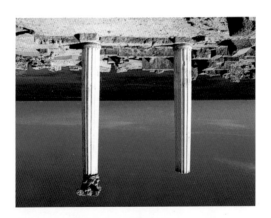

saRDinia

INSIGHT **POCKET GUIDE**